A MANIFESTO FOR
SOCIAL CHANGE

Moeletsi Mbeki & Nobantu Mbeki

A MANIFESTO FOR SOCIAL CHANGE

How to Save South Africa

PICADOR AFRICA

First published in 2016 by Picador Africa,
an imprint of Pan Macmillan South Africa
Private Bag X19, Northlands
Johannesburg 2116

www.panmacmillan.co.za

ISBN 978-1-77010-497-6
eBook ISBN 978-1-77010-498-3

Design and typesetting by Triple M Design, Johannesburg
Cover design by K4

Printed and bound by Bidvest Data, Cape Town

CONTENTS

FIGURES

PREFACE

A Manifesto for Social Change: How to Save South Africa is the third of a three-volume series that started seven years ago investigating the causes of our country's – and the continent's – development obstacles.

The first volume, *Architects of Poverty: Why African Capitalism Needs Changing*, was published in 2009. In that book I set out to explain what role African elites played in creating and promoting their fellow Africans' misery.

The second book, which I edited, was published in 2011. *Advocates for Change: How to Overcome Africa's Challenges* set out to show that there were short- to medium-term solutions for many of Africa's and South Africa's problems, from agriculture to healthcare, if only the powers that be would take note. *Advocates for Change* was a response to readers of *Architects of Poverty* wanting to hear more about solutions for our continent's problems.

A Manifesto for Social Change: How to Save South Africa has been written more than 20 years after the end of apartheid and the birth of a new South Africa. Since the advent of democracy, a new society has come into existence and taken shape. Working with Nobantu, this book set out to investigate the phenomenon of the 'gridlocked' nature of our society and to unpack the various elements at the root of this current crisis. But the research led us to inescapable conclusions about how the social structure of South Africa functions and what is needed to save the country and take it forward in a way that is sustainable for all its citizens.

Under the apartheid system we knew who the winners were and who the losers were. Under the new democratic system, who are the new winners and who are the new losers? On page 35 you will find a diagram illustrating how the new society functions. Five social classes are identified, illustrating how many working-age people belong to each class. The largest class is what we call the 'underclass' and the second-largest is the 'middle class/political elite'; there are no prizes for guessing the winners or the losers.

I need to thank a number of people who contributed to

making this trilogy possible. Firstly, the managing director of Pan Macmillan South Africa, Terry Morris, who approached me some years ago to compile the newspaper articles I had been writing since 1990 into a book. This led to *Architects of Poverty*, most of which ended up being new material. Secondly, I must thank the contributors to *Advocates for Change* for their insightful chapters in this important book. And thirdly, I must thank my niece and co-author, Nobantu Mbeki, for persevering with this current project through all the twists and turns that it has taken. Nobantu was, in fact, the first person to see the possibility of a book in the social structure of South Africa diagram. Finally, a very special thank you to Pali Lehohla, South Africa's Statistician General, who worked out the numbers of how many working-age people belong to each social class.

Moeletsi Mbeki
March 2016

CHAPTER 1

AN OVERVIEW OF SOUTH AFRICA TODAY

'During my lifetime I have dedicated myself to the struggle of the African people. I have fought against white domination, and I have fought against black domination. I have cherished the ideal of a democratic and free society in which all persons live together in harmony and with equal opportunities. It is an ideal which I hope to live for and to achieve. But if needs be, it is an ideal for which I am prepared to die.'

– Nelson Mandela speaking at the Rivonia Trial, 1963–64, at the conclusion of which he and six fellow freedom fighters were sentenced to life imprisonment

Millions of people throughout the world helped bring down apartheid in South Africa. Besides their abhorrence of racism, they looked hopefully toward the emergence of a just and equitable society. In the wise, forgiving and larger-than-life personality of Nelson Mandela the world imagined a South Africa at peace with itself, ready to make the necessary sacrifices to build the first truly modern country in Africa.

But more than two decades later, the country appears to be retreating further and further from this vision. Almost all the hallmarks that were associated with the old, repressive, white minority regime seem to remain in place:

- A brutal police force that has gunned down demonstrators for demanding a better life.
- Arrogant mining companies that exploit the country's natural resources, leaving behind only a trail of environmental hazards.
- Rampant infectious diseases decimating hundreds of thousands of black lives.
- Millions of young people condemned to a futureless existence by a failed education system.
- Growing inequality, especially amongst blacks.
- Rampant corruption that has put South Africa at 61 out of 168 countries in the 2015 Transparency International Corruption Perception Index.

The list seems endless. Old South Africa lives on. And now the situation has reached boiling point.

Why revolutions happen

Sooner or later all societies are faced with the challenge of how they should modernise themselves so that they can meet the new and changing expectations of their populations. During the 18th century the French people's growing expectations for greater economic and political freedom were frustrated by the monarchy and aristocracy who controlled political power and the state. This inevitably led to the social and political explosions known as the French Revolution. At about the same time, nearer to home, was the Shaka revolution, which swept aside independent clans and led to the creation of a more productive feudal society that could sustain a state with a standing army.

Yearning for industrial development in the 19th century, Americans were confronted by the obstacle of slavery in the southern states, a system based on export of raw materials such as cotton and tobacco. At great cost, the Civil War was fought between the North and South, leading to the abolition of slavery in 1865. Within a generation, the American economy become the largest and most sophisticated economy in the world, overtaking that of Great Britain.

3

The most successful modernisation initiative of recent years was the opening up to the world by China in the late 1970s. The changes transformed the Asian country from a backwater to the second-largest economy in the world while simultaneously raising hundreds of millions of its people out of poverty.

What is often overlooked by the admirers of China's achievements, however, is the turmoil that preceded and therefore facilitated the changes that would happen. China's developmental achievements would not have been possible without the upheavals of the Cultural Revolution, which greatly weakened the Communist Party, and the death of Mao Zedong and the defeat of his anointed heirs, the Gang of Four, by Deng Xiaoping and his faction. China's modernisation was a result of a conflict triggered by expectations for higher living standards unfulfilled during the Maoist era, which lasted from 1949 to 1976.

This is where South Africa now finds itself.

In the early 1990s South Africa accomplished universal suffrage, a process that took nearly a century and a half following the introduction of the property ownership qualified franchise in the Cape in 1854. So what was achieved in 1994, after the painful and costly 140-year struggle against reactionary and anti-democratic forces? Majority rule. In practice, that meant political power was transferred from a white oligarchy to a coalition led by the black nationalist middle class who, in partnership with organised labour, the churches and civil society organisations, had led the fight for democracy in South Africa. With this transfer of political power, and therefore control of the state, the slaughter of innocent black people was brought to an end, as was the police state that had been the main protector of white minority interests.

Rule of law – frozen since the National Party come to power in 1948 – became South Africa's mode of operation. Every citizen's rights were stipulated in a generally accepted constitution. At the broader socio-economic level, it led to the mushrooming of a new black middle class that was needed to man the many departments and parastatals of the new democratic government. Even the white oligarchy that controlled the economy for over a hundred years suddenly discovered that it needed black partners. They, too, frantically recruited black shareholders into their businesses' ownership structures as well as black professionals into their managerial cadre. For the black blue-collar workers, however, it was business as usual. Whatever gains they made they continued to fight for, negotiating with their employers as they had been doing since the legalisation of black trade unions in the late 1970s.

But not only did democracy open up domestic politics

5

to broader participation, it opened up the South African economy to competition from the big wide world. Since the end of the Second World War, the South African economy had been protected by high tariff walls, which attracted foreign companies to set up subsidiaries inside those walls, thus driving the growth of the country's manufacturing industries. These foreign investors gave South Africa the veneer that it was a modernising country whose only problem was its government's archaic apartheid policies. These foreign companies and their South African counterparts told the world to be patient, assuring them apartheid would inevitably be eroded by increasing industrialisation and the urbanisation of the black population.

As repression in South Africa intensified, sanctions imposed by several Western governments led to the transfer and/or sale of many of these foreign-owned subsidiaries to South African companies, further strengthening the hold of the white oligarchy over the country's economy.

Class and state

These developments consolidated the already enormous economic power wielded by what is popularly known as the Minerals-Energy Complex (MEC). Unsurprisingly, the protracted constitutional negotiations, which lasted from

6

1986 to 1996, carefully skirted questions about how to address the vast systemic poverty that mining, agriculture and physical infrastructure development had generated through the infamous migrant labour system.

It was a lone Stellenbosch University economist, Sampie Terreblanche, who raised this important issue with the Truth and Reconciliation Commission, to the great annoyance of the South Africa's captains of industry. At the time, Terreblanche proposed a wealth tax on rich whites, but the suggestion was brushed aside by the commissioners as speaking out of turn. The choice to shelve the issue of poverty has continued to haunt our nation.

Today the largest social class in South Africa comprises people living in poverty. Through the weight of their numbers, it is the underclass who decides who gets elected. As the majority they should be among the country's key decision-makers. Instead they get crumbs from the government in the form of social welfare grants.

This is why South Africa has arrived at the crossroads that the French arrived at in 1789, the Americans in 1860 and the Chinese in 1978. The great majority of South Africans today expect economic changes that go beyond social welfare programmes. They want to control their own lives; they want to provide for their families through their own efforts and not through the largesse of the state or philanthropists.

More than two years since Nelson Mandela died and 22 years after the first democratic elections, South Africans are still struggling to achieve the ideal that he and his fellow Rivonia trialists cherished. And slowly but surely the fault lines have begun to show along their Long Walk to Freedom. The cost of these deviations are becoming evident every day and have started playing out throughout South African society, with growing signs that the gains of the past 22 years of freedom are reversible. Tensions between the classes are rising at an alarming rate.

The main political dynamic of South Africa today is that the state is trying to increase its power relative to civil society – that is the part of the population that earns its livelihood outside government, including business, religious and social organisations, academia and the media. Civil society has a vested interest in democracy; the state, however, is more interested in reducing the autonomy of civil society while increasing its own power.

The post-1994 democratic regime initially kept the social peace by adopting a 'live and let live' approach towards civil society, especially its business element. But this approach made it impossible for the emerging black elite to make money and acquire assets in order to become a real, propertied class instead of being mere employees of the state. The Auditor General's annual reports constantly reveal wasteful and

8

unauthorised expenditures by state organisations. Hidden in these unauthorised and wasteful expenditures are corrupt self-enrichment acts by state employees.

Still, South Africa has strengths that should see it through the turbulent times ahead. The country's political system, which was negotiated by most of its stakeholders – domestic and foreign – enjoys considerable legitimacy with the people; the Constitution is considered to be sacrosanct by the majority of South Africans.

But the legitimacy of a political system is one thing, the day-to-day management of it is another – and the management of the political system by the ANC government leaves much to be desired. The political administration is hugely incompetent, resulting in extensive dissatisfaction especially among poor black South Africans. Public sector managers from the highest (politicians) to the lowest (civil servants in local government) are increasingly perceived to be corrupt; they are seen as more concerned with enriching themselves than with providing the services they are elected and employed to do.

The perceived mismanagement is leading to conflicts between the black poor and working class on one side and the state on the other. For example, according to a Media24 report from 13 May 2013, former Gauteng police commissioner, Lt-Gen Mzwandile Petros revealed at a press conference that over a five-week period during April and May that year, there were 650 protests in Gauteng alone and 40 of those were violent, resulting in damage to property and injuries to both police and protestors. The incompetence and corruption of the current administration, which continues to be highlighted by the rampant service delivery protests throughout the country, creates the state's main vulnerability notwithstanding the legitimacy of its political system.

Its second source of vulnerability is the economic system. Unlike the political system, the economic system – which was inherited from more than 350 years of South Africa's evolution – was not negotiated by the country's stakeholders. South Africa's economic system therefore does not enjoy universal acceptance. The negotiations that led to the restructuring of the political system studiously sidestepped issues pertaining to the restructuring of the economic system. At the time this was probably a wise decision as there was little consensus both among the main stakeholders, and in some instances within the different stakeholders, what needed to be done.

Now the need to modernise the South African economy so that it is inclusive and grows is past urgent. But the vested interests of foreign and domestic economic oligarchy that control the MEC, as well as the African nationalist elite that control the state, are major obstacles toward this restructuring.

Challenges facing the cherished ideal

All of this isn't to suggest that nothing has been achieved in the last two decades of freedom. The country has:

- ❏ Retained the pre-existing economic system virtually intact, especially the independent private sector, trade unions and civil society in general.
- ❏ Expanded the upper end of the black middle classes, mainly through state employment.
- ❏ Raised the standards of living of the black poor through the rapid extension of social welfare.
- ❏ Maintained limited forms of representative democracy – proportional representation with closed party lists, but no electoral constituencies.

What is deeply concerning is that these achievements are reversible. In addition to growing inequality and discontent, along with the very real threat of a police state, fault lines include:

- ❏ Increasing challenges to the independence of South Africa's important and strategic civil society by the new black political elite who want to use the state for their private enrichment.

11

❏ An unchanged economic structure that continues to be dominated by mining, energy and finance capital, which has locked the country's economy into a low-growth trajectory.

❏ A state that is increasingly aligning itself with anti-democracy regimes and shunning pro-democracy ones with scant regard, if any, to South Africa's economic self-interest.

How these very real threats are acting out will determine the county's increasingly bleak future.

The state versus the black poor

There are several European countries, such as Spain and Greece, with high unemployment levels. But these do not translate into political risks per se. South Africa's economic woes, however, translate into major political risk factors because of the relationship between South Africa's leading political party, the ANC, and its key electorate, the black poor.

The ANC is increasingly at war with the black poor who form the backbone of its electorate. The most dramatic example of this war was the fatal shooting of 34 low-paid miners and the wounding of a further 78 on 16 August 2012 at the Marikana platinum mine.

12

According to an Ipsos survey of who voted for the ANC in the last general elections in 2014, 64% did not work and nearly half had not completed high school.

Figure 1.1 **Education and working status of ANC voters, 2009 elections**

Level of education	All ANC voters %
No education	7
Up to some high school	62
Matric	23
Tertiary education/other	8

Working status	%
Working full-time	24
Working part-time	9
Do not work	67

Source: Ipsos Markinor.

Figure 1.2 **Education and working status of ANC voters, 2014 elections**

Level of education	All ANC voters %
No education	4
Up to some high school	46
Matric	41
Tertiary education/other	9

Working status	%
Working full-time	25
Working part-time	11
Do not work	64

Source: Ipsos Markinor.

Why do the black poor vote for the ANC and, most importantly, what will happen when they stop doing so?

13

This question goes to the heart of the stability issues facing South Africa. The simple answer, which explains the growing risk perception of the country, is that there is no clear answer. Will the ANC willingly give up power to its political competitors? Will it follow in the footsteps of ZANU(PF) in Zimbabwe and resort to violence and machinations to stay in power? Will it use a combination of violence and populist economic enticements for the black poor and dirty tricks and violence against its rivals? All these scenarios are possible and, importantly, feasible.

Under these circumstances, who is going to make long-term investment in an environment where there are such unfathomable uncertainties or 'known unknowns', to borrow a phrase from former United States Secretary of Defense Donald Rumsfeld? The answer is that no one in the private sector, whether South African or foreign, will invest in such an uncertain political environment, especially after so many South African and European investors got burnt in neighbouring Zimbabwe.

Only those investors who already have assets in South Africa and have to keep their operations ticking over will continue to make more investments. And with investment running below 20% of GDP annually, according to the International Monetary Fund Global Economic Outlook 2011, it would appear that investors are only maintaining

14

their existing assets rather than making new significant investments or expanding existing ones.

The state could be a serious potential investor but by virtue of its own ideology and survival imperatives, it is locked into promoting black consumption rather than investment.

The consumption revolution

At the end of apartheid, the economy, which had been labouring under a multiplicity of sanctions, started to grow, creating an atmosphere of optimism about South Africa's future to local and international investors as well as to the population at large.

The years from 1996 to 2008 saw a steep rise in the international prices of minerals, South Africa's main export. The expectation was that the new commodities super-cycle driven by the industrialisation of China and other big Asian countries had begun, and was expected to last for several decades. The new ANC government saw this period of impending prosperity as an ideal time for it to reward its political constituency, black South Africa – both in the form of civil service as well as social welfare grants – with accelerated private household consumption, as the following graphs illustrate.

15

Figure 1.3 **Public and private sector pay index**

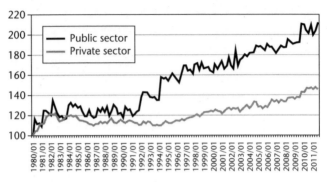

Source: Economists.co.za.

Figure 1.4 **Social grant recipients, 2008–2013: Q2**

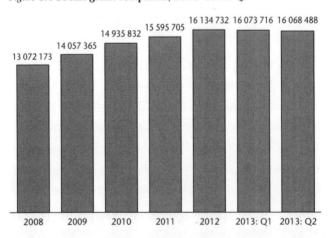

Source: SASSA Annual Report, various years; SASSA Statistical Report: Fact Sheet
no.1 of 2013 (www.sassa.gov.za).

16

In order to promote private household consumption, the ANC government took a number of bold policy initiatives. First, it slashed tariff protection for South African industries to cheapen consumer goods in the domestic market. According to a 2006 report out of the University of Cape Town's Southern African Labour and Development Research Unit, the simple average tariff rate, inclusive of surcharges, fell from 22% in 1994 to 7.9% by 2004. Second, it embarked on the building of a vast welfare state for the black poor via a system of increased social grants. The number of cash social welfare recipients increased from R2 million in 1996 to R13 million in 2008 and R16 million in 2013. And third, it built up a massive state bureaucracy that was paid salaries that became the envy of civil servants in the developed world.

For example, the president of South Africa earned R2.6 million in 2012 compared to the German chancellor's R2.3 million and the prime minister of the United Kingdom who earned R1.8 million.

For many years, manufacturing was the largest employer in the South African economy. This has changed under the ANC government. According to its June 2014 Quarterly Employment Statistics survey, there were 455 701 national government employees, a further 1 118 748 people working for provincial authorities, 311 361 people were employed by local authorities and 275 851 employees worked for 'other government institutions', such as libraries, parks, zoos and education and training authorities. This adds up to a grand total of 2.161 million civil servants.

Not to be outdone, South Africa's private sector came up with its own wealth redistribution policy: BEE. The theory was that since black people had been deprived of access to wealth for virtually all of the century, private business had to make its own contribution to redress this injustice. What happened in practice was that private corporations used BEE to co-opt former black resistance leaders as well as many leaders of black trade unions, creating a class of idle, rich ANC politicians who were soon to sharpen their skills in intrigue and as allies of South Africa's big business.

All these initiatives by the ANC government and the private sector unleashed a consumption revolution that was partly funded by improved tax collection and the creation of credit. Large international retailers, bankers and fast-food companies started investing in these sectors.

This consumption revolution has been disastrous for South Africa's productive economy. First, it transfers resources through taxation from the production sector to government and to private household consumption, thereby starving the production sector of resources to invest. The result has been to drive up unemployment while creating the illusion of economic growth, which in reality was driven by rises in commodity prices. Second, low levels of investment inevitably led to higher levels of imports as what is being consumed is increasingly not produced domestically.

Faced with a double burden – the economy being starved of capital investment and being weighed down by debt – what did the employed people of South Africa do? They borrowed. They borrowed so they could pay their taxes in order to keep the government operating; they borrowed to pay school fees for their children; they borrowed to feed the unemployed; they borrowed to pay for toll roads.

Government also got in on the game and borrowed. It borrowed to pay for the lavish salaries and allowances of its ministers and senior officials. It borrowed to pay for the infrastructure that the people could not afford to pay to use. It borrowed to hire more people to collect unpaid service charges and to prosecute and disconnect those who are perennial offenders. According to one estimate, Telkom disconnects about as many of the new telephone lines as it builds.

During the commodity boom years of 2002 to 2011 South Africa's mining sector actually shrank by 1% annually, according to Canada's Fraser Institute, the leading think tank on the global mining industry. This was mainly blamed on the unpredictability and infrastructure shortcomings of the South African government's mining policy.

19

Over the past the 22 years of ANC rule, a phenomenon similar to the action of an opening pair of scissors has started to occur. On the one hand, a new, well-off class made up of black politicians, senior civil servants and BEE beneficiaries emerged and, growing quite rapidly, it joined the ranks of the existing white professional, middle and upper classes. Moving simultaneously but in the opposite direction, black blue-collar workers started losing jobs in most sectors of the real economy, especially in agriculture, mining and manufacturing. Where there was blue-collar job growth, this took the form of casual work, especially in the private security sector. Under these circumstances it was a matter of time before conflict between blue-collar workers, their employers and the ANC government would break out.

Blue-collar workers in South Africa's production industries, especially mining and agriculture, were left behind by the consumption revolution that favoured the middle class of all races and the black poor. It was therefore only a matter of time before the country's blue-collar workers were going to respond to their exclusion from the gravy train. In this regard, the angry strikes in the mining and agriculture sectors during 2012 should not have come as a surprise.

South Africa's black poor have also started showing impatience in the growing service delivery protests and the government has started preparing for the inevitable showdown. These preparations include:

❏ Militarisation of the police.
❏ Preparations for the suppression of freedom of the media.
❏ Manipulation of judicial processes and personnel.
❏ Purges of members of the party who propose alternative policies.
❏ Refusal to introduce a constituency-based electoral system to complement proportional representation.
❏ Strengthening the powers of chiefs over the rural population.

As we have demonstrated above, the ANC government has been pursuing economic policies that have helped it get elected. These policies have, however, gradually created major problems for the viability for the country's economy as the population is living beyond its means. The larger problem is that these policies are, at best, reinforcing existing structural imbalances and, at worst, actively creating new ones. These self-defeating policies are ironically leading the government into a collision course with many sectors of society.

There is something very, very wrong with South Africa. And when we say something is wrong with South Africa, there is something very wrong with how the political elite are managing South Africa.

Consumer capitalism versus globalisation

So what does its future look like?

During the last two decades South Africa's real output in manufacturing has been in a nosedive. Manufacturing, probably more than any other sector of the economy, has been shrinking fast. Its production equipment is aging and, in some industries, is ancient. Most of South Africa's cement-manufacturing equipment is, on average, 30 years or older. Not surprisingly, it could not cope when it had to supply cement to construction companies to build new stadiums for the 2010 FIFA World Cup.

The mining industry, which is at the heart of the South African economy, is also shrinking. Not because we have run out of minerals but because the industry is addicted to cheap, essentially free, labour; mining worked when there was indenture. We ran out of electricity in 2008 because the ANC government had not bothered to build new power stations to meet growing demand.

Increasingly, South Africa is consuming imports: milk, chicken, beef, shoes, clothes and cement, to name but a few products. We pay for all of this by selling our minerals, mostly in a raw state, to foreigners and by borrowing from our banks and also from foreigners – another reason we describe the ANC's version of capitalism as a mode of consumption rather than a mode of production.

Low levels of investment in some sectors of the economy and in some industriess makes South Africa extremely vulnerable to international competition, which is implicit in globalisation.

One of the most important drivers of economic development in today's world, globalisation has contributed to raising the standards of living of hundreds of millions of people, particularly in Asia. It has also helped to keep down the living costs of many in the developed world and kept their populations employed in the services and manufacturing industries that help to drive production industries in Asia.

Globalisation, however, has its casualties. Its main casualties are in middle-income countries such as South Africa, which had achieved a significant level of industrialisation prior to the opening up of the Chinese, Indian and former Soviet bloc economies over the past 30 years or so.

One of the main drivers of globalisation was the low cost and abundant labour of Asia and Eastern Europe, which was combined with the advanced production technologies developed by Western countries. This combination enabled the world's multinational corporations to produce high-quality products cheaply for world markets.

The crises middle-income countries faced was that their pre-existing industries had comparatively old technology, higher labour and management costs and entrenched industrial relations practices. This combination made it difficult to compete against manufactured products in low-labour-cost Asian countries. In many instances these countries did not even have trade unions to protect workers against poor employment conditions.

South Africa is a good example of a middle-income country that is sinking steadily under the weight of globalisation. Between the First World War and the early 1980s, South Africa had achieved a fair degree of industrialisation. The development of the mining sector during this period led to the growth of related manufacturing industries such as chemicals, iron, steel and engineering as well as agriculture to feed the rapidly growing urban population. A wide range of consumption goods industries – textile, clothing, footwear and motor vehicles – also developed during this period.

Now many of the industries created prior to the 1980s are struggling to compete against cheaper imports. Whereas manufacturing industries made up over 25% of South Africa's GDP in the 1980s and were the largest employers of labour, today manufacturing accounts for less than 10% of GDP and employs fewer people than the state. This explains another

24

negative trend: South Africa's regression into a raw materials and metals exporter.

Going hand in hand with South Africa's de-industrialisation is the decline of its mining sector (for further discussion of how industries undermine development, see Chapter 4). Because of predatory policies towards the mining sector by the ANC government – through BEE, taxation and mining rights policies – new investment in the mining sector has all but dried up. As a result, South African mines, despite the country's vast mineral endowment, are employing fewer and fewer people; are becoming deeper; have become the focus of violent conflicts between government, employers, the workers and among workers; and play an increasingly important role in capital flight. As the mines go deeper and become more conflict ridden, they become more mechanised in the process, employing fewer workers.

Commenting to the *Financial Times* in 2014 on demands for higher pay by trade unions in the platinum mining sector, Johan Theron, the executive in charge of corporate relations for Implats, the second-largest platinum mining company in South Africa, remarked:

Amcu [Association of Mineworkers and Construction Union] is not merely seeking an inflation-linked cost of living wage increase. It is calling for a complete recalibration of the labour

25

system in South Africa. No business can be forced into such deep structural changes that are clearly unaffordable and unsustainable and will have dire consequences if implemented. They will have far-reaching consequences, one of which will be a renewed focus on mechanisation to achieve the labour productivity that will make these wages sustainable.

Theron went on to warn that the number of mineworkers 'will decrease drastically'. His observations were reiterated by another Implats executive, Gerhard Potgieter, who said:

With the labour-intensive mines struggling the way they are, it will be difficult to convince any board or investor that labour-intensive operations are the way to go. We as mining companies are forced into saying that in the future we will mine in mechanised ways or not mine at all because we can't see a way that labour-intensive methods will be profitable.

The *Financial Mail* went on to report that in the coming five years, Implats plans on shutting down nine, old mined-out shafts and replacing their production with three new shafts that the company intends starting. A fourth shaft, known as Leeuwkop, is already in the process of being developed and will be mechanised so that instead of employing 10 000 workers it will employ just 3 000.

The downgrades

There is a growing consensus that, amongst emerging markets, South Africa is becoming riskier. Together with Venezuela, Argentina, Ukraine and Greece, South Africa is in the top five most painful economies in the world to live and work in according to Bloomberg's latest Misery Index.

Downgrading South Africa's sovereign credit rating from BBB+ to BBB, rating agency Fitch pulled no punches in its January 2013 statement:

> Social and political tensions have increased as subdued growth, coupled with rising corruption and worsening government effectiveness, has constrained the government's ability to improve living standards, reduce the 25.5% unemployment rate and redress historical inequalities as rapidly as the population demands. Protests over poor service delivery increased to record levels in 2012 and the economy has been beset with violent strikes that have affected growth and the current account.

South Africa consistently has the highest rate of unemployment, consistently hovering in the region of 25%. Even comparing South African unemployment rates to those in sub-Saharan Africa, the same picture emerges. For example, youth unemployment (people between the ages of 15 and 24) stands at 48% in South Africa compared to an average of only 11% in the rest of sub-Saharan Africa.

Moody's, another international rating agency, gave a fuller explanation of why it downgraded South Africa from Baa1 to A3 with its negative outlook back in September 2012. The following is an extract:

> The main driver for the downgrade of South Africa's ratings is Moody's lowered assessment of institutional strength to 'moderate' from 'high,' an important factor in the rating agency's judgment of a sovereign's economic resiliency. The revision reflects Moody's view of the South African authorities' reduced capacity to handle the current political and economic situation and to implement effective strategies that could place the economy on a path to faster and more inclusive growth. While the National Development Plan submitted by the country's National Planning Commission last November formulated a comprehensive set of reforms meant to lead to increased development and reduced inequality, Moody's notes that the fractious domestic environment is not conducive to the reforms being implemented at present. An example is the protracted debate once again of the proposal to introduce the subsidy for younger workers, who face a 50%

unemployment rate, at June's National Policy Conference.

The second key driver for the downgrade is the reduced room for manoeuvre for counter-cyclical macroeconomic policy in light of the persistent deterioration in the government debt metrics over the past four years, as the rise in the wage bill and debt servicing costs reduces the amount of resources available for development spending. With government debt at around 40% of GDP, the fiscal space that had been created before the global crisis has now largely dissipated. The government is working towards a stabilisation of the debt-to-GDP ratio through increased spending discipline, which by moving the primary budget balance out of deficit would eventually restore some of the lost fiscal space.

However, Moody's notes that these plans were recently rendered more challenging after the recent wage agreement with public-sector workers. Although the government had planned to rein in wage increases to 6% per annum over the next three years, the settlement was far more generous, thereby partially eroding the government's contingency reserve and probably reducing the ability to fill public sector job vacancies going forward.

The third driver informing Moody's decision to downgrade South Africa's sovereign rating is the more negative investment climate, which has been aggravated in recent years by shortfalls in energy, transportation and other infrastructure as

29

well as high labour costs relative to productivity. In addition, investors' awareness of the country's long-standing socio-economic challenges, in particular the high unemployment rate and continuing wide income disparities nearly 20 years after the democratic transition, have been heightened following recent developments in the mining sector. Since the South African economy has a low savings rate, it is heavily dependent on foreign portfolio inflows to finance its rather large current account deficits. These non-debt-creating inflows have reliably funded the external deficits for many years, allowing the build-up of substantial foreign-exchange reserves at the central bank and significantly reducing the country's external vulnerability.

Moody's cautioned that any reversal of those flows could be accommodated because of the flexibility of the exchange rate, the liquidity of the equity market and the foreign reserves cushion. However, they wrote, economic growth would be further constrained in the unlikely event that foreign capital inflows shrunk substantially.

The rating outlook remains negative because of uncertainty as to whether the policy decisions being devised ahead of the December leadership conference of the ANC will be helpful or detrimental to the country's growth and competitiveness outlook. The ANC's recommendations following the June policy conference called for 'more radical policies and decisive action to effect thorough-going socio-economic and continued democratic transformation', suggesting that increasingly interventionist strategies are highly likely. To the extent that such strategies would deter private investment and incoming capital to South Africa, they could further diminish its growth potential at a difficult period in the global economy.

In December 2015, Fitch downgraded South Africa to one notch above sub-investment grade, normally referred to as junk rating. Their main reasons were:

❏ The continued crises in the supply of electricity.
❏ Growing government debt, expected to increase to 50% of GDP at the end of the financial year 2015/16.
❏ Persistent current account deficit, despite weak domestic demand and sharp decline of the rand.
❏ Unemployment remains stubbornly high, at 25.5%, with the share of the working age population in unemployment at a mere 43.8%.

31

CHAPTER 2

THE DYNAMICS OF A STUNTED CAPITALIST SOCIETY

In his studies of the nature of inequality over long periods of time, Thomas Piketty identified the centrality of political power as the determinant of how economic benefits are distributed in a given society. It was no accident that in his seminal book *Capital in the 21st Century*, Piketty literally set the scene for global inequality in South Africa, where he described the massacres of striking platinum miners at Marikana on 16 August 2012. As he states repeatedly throughout the book, inequality it is neither God given nor spawned by forces of nature; inequality and its counterparts, especially social conflicts, are an outcome of the social structure of a particular country.

Understanding the social structure of South Africa is therefore central not only to addressing our inequality and its deep conflicts but to understanding why our country's economy barely grows, dogged by high levels of unemployment and poverty.

As we have established below, South Africa has five core social classes: the economic elite, the political elite, blue-collar workers, the underclass and unemployed and the independent professionals and those who work for non-profit organisations.

What is most striking about the social structure of South Africa is that the largest social class is the underclass. This tells the stark story: of the estimated 23.6 million South Africans over the age of 15 in 2014, a full half fall into the category of the underclass, the bulk of whom are unemployed. Since the informal sector employs relatively few, others are subsidised by relatives who work, as well as by the state through welfare transfers. This in part explains South Africa's massive inequality.

Figure 2.1 is a schematic presentation of South Africa's social structure, which grew out of the mode of the exploitation of the country's mineral resources. We describe South Africa as a stunted capitalist society because its economy is unable

Figure 2.1 Social structure of South Africa

Social group	Main strengths	Key weaknesses	Vulnerability
ECONOMIC ELITE **Core objectives:** Maximise profits and retain ownership of assets	Own productive assets and control skilled management	Do not control government; dependence on state-owned power and transport companies	Asset seizures; onerous taxation; exposed to corruption by political elite; mismanagement of economy
POLITICAL ELITE **Core objectives:** Maximise consumption for black middle class and constituency and retain monopoly of political power	Control state and manage government revenues	Dependence on vote of underclass; do not own productive assets; doubtful management skills	Change of allegiance of underclass; political activism of economic elite; opposition from blue-collar workers; capital flight
BLUE-COLLAR WORKERS *Formal sector* **Core objectives:** Expand trade union membership and raise remuneration	Own labour power and control independent trade unions	Threat from large overhang of unemployed	Mismanagement of economy; corruption; loss of influence with government; political intimidation by ruling party agents
UNDERCLASS/ UNEMPLOYED *Informal sector* **Core objectives:** Survive and influence state	Large numbers and voting power	Lack artisan skills; dependence on government welfare	Economic meltdown and political manipulation
INDEPENDENT PROFESSIONALS/ NON-PROFIT ORGANISATIONS AND NEW ENTREPRENEURS **Core objectives:** Freedom of association and speech and reduce state interference	Command many skills and extensive influence through religion and good works	Fragmented and lack of cohesion; financial dependence on donors	Donor unpredictability; intimidation by government agents; over-cautious banks

Source: Moeletsi Mbeki.

35

to absorb in a productive way nearly half of its working age population. A society in which almost half of its adult population is literally pensioned off cannot develop in a significant way.

Figure 2.2 below was produced with the help of Statistics South Africa, which has allowed us to provide the numerical membership of each class, which roughly corresponds to the table above. Note that the elite and the middle class are divided into economic and political segments, respectively representing those working in the private sector and those working in the service of the state.

Figure 2.2 **Breakdown of social classes: 2014**

	Total	Percentage
Elite		.44
Economic	84 766	
Political	20 270	
Middle class		9.79
Economic	1 556 502	
Political	753 984	
Blue-collar workers	9 005 460	38.15
Underclass and unemployed	11 755 744	49.79
Independent professionals and NPOs	431 517	1.83

Source: Statistics South Africa.

Capitalist class: The economic elite

The strength of the capitalist class is that it owns the country's productive assets – the banks and the mines – but, most importantly, it controls the highest levels of skills that we have. The managers, engineers and accountants who run private sector corporations are also part of the economic elite. However, the economic elite has a key weakness in that it does not control the state. This means that countless opportunities for holdup arise. For example, it is dependent on the state for electric power and for rail transport and for its ports. In South Africa, where industries are in the centre of the country rather than at the coast, the issue of who controls the transport system becomes crucial; the political elite can use transport infrastructure as a mechanism for taxing the private sector.

This raises the key question of why South Africa's economic elite would not invest in this type of capacity, effectively tantamount to achieving some autonomy and a measure of independence from the constraints imposed by the state, intentional or otherwise. South Africa's economic elite has major vulnerabilities. Some wounds are self-inflicted, but others are not. The former vulnerabilities mean that it intentionally scales down its participation or exposure to this economy because it now finds itself in a

37

position in which it cannot act with its prior impunity. The latter determine the recurrently suppressed investment into privately increasing capacity in this economy. Its primary present vulnerability is to asset seizure by those who control political power. This could take many forms: nationalisation, BEE or indigenisation policies, onerous taxation or old-fashioned corruption, such as bribes in return for government licences.

The capitalist class has developed ways of defending itself. Moving capital out of South Africa is one way. A 2011 study in the *Journal of Southern African Studies* found that, as a percentage of GDP, capital flight rose at an average of 5.4% per year between 1980 and 1993 to 9.3% between 1994 and 2000, and 12% between 2001 and 2007, finally hitting a staggering 20% of GDP in 2007.

This begins to express that South Africa is an economy in structural decline. The insecurity of the owners of capital is one of the central development problems South Africa has and it is a major contributor to the stunted capitalist society. This however merely exacerbates what precipitated this in the first instance: a capitalist class that now has to account to society at large in a way it has never had to before. This is one key cause of gridlock.

A property-less political elite

During the last 100 years, we have had two types of dominant political elites: the first was clustered around Afrikaner nationalism and the second was clustered around African nationalism. What distinguished them was not that one was white and the other black. It was that one elite, the Afrikaner nationalists, comprised property owners, mainly landowners. The other elite, the African nationalists, did not. They were mainly professionals of one description or another, but they were not property owners.

So how do the attributes of property ownership and lack of property ownership manifest themselves in the development of society? We have created a schematic presentation of how the elite who own property survive, how this group looks after itself, how it reproduces itself and how it organises society.

The Afrikaner elite, the dominant elite between 1910 and 1994, were property owners and owners of productive assets. Their private consumption was essentially funded from profits that came initially from agriculture and from the exploitation of labour in agriculture.

The Seed is Mine, a fascinating book by Charles van Onselen, tells a graphic story about the exploitation of sharecroppers who were nominal partners of the landowners in the former

39

222222222222

Figure 2.3 **Nationalism in Africa**

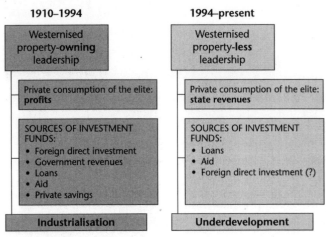

Source: Moeletsi Mbeki.

Boer republics. Labour tenants, for example, formed ways of creating profit for the owners of land, the dominant elite to which the British handed political power in 1910.

When the political elite reproduced itself by profit, then society had a number of resources that were not being consumed and this could go into investment. When the dominant political elite survived on profits, then government revenues, loans to the state, foreign aid, and private savings went into investment, primarily to make the land assets of the dominant elite more profitable and to advance the collective agenda of this portion of society. This, however,

40

nominally became a communal endowment when political power changed hands.

For example, today we have over 20 000 km of railway network in South Africa. A huge part of that network was created in order to service the agriculture sector under the National Party government. So we had the development of infrastructure to make the productive assets of the political elite more productive and more profitable, which was why we had the partial industrialisation of South Africa that we see today.

The elite who took power after 1994 did not own productive assets, so their consumption has been financed through state revenues. Broadly speaking, this is what has happened throughout much of sub-Saharan Africa: the use of state revenues to finance the private consumption of elites means ever-increasing direct and indirect taxes.

The consequence of diverting resources to the private consumption of the elite is that we have fewer and fewer funds available for investment to create employment. Today, one-third of GDP goes to government spending and more than half of that spending goes into salaries and social welfare. Above and beyond the private funding of investment by shrinking enterprises of scale in South Africa, the only resources that are available for productive investment are loans, foreign direct investment and foreign aid. It should therefore come as no surprise that South Africa has one of the highest unemployment levels in the world.

Blue-collar workers

In the South African situation of a stunted capitalist society, blue-collar workers are not what Karl Marx said the proletariat would be under capitalism – the grave diggers of the capitalists' system. Under conditions of stunted capitalism, blue-collar workers are a minority caught in the middle of two powerful forces. On one side are the bourgeois political elite who, with the support of the underclass, control the state. On the other side is the capitalist class which, backed by the powerful managerial class, control the economy. Blue-collar workers, caught in the middle, are the ham in the sandwich. The South Africa environment actually reverses Karl Marx's prediction in that stunted capitalism, as we shall see, is the grave digger of the proletariat.

In South Africa, the blue-collar worker stands to benefit the most from an industrial revolution. These are those currently at work whose prospects are increasingly tenuous. If we understand blue-collar workers as endangered, then it should be apparent that we have not begun to understand the consequences of the de-industrialisation of the South African economy for this society at large. At the very least, re-industrialisation would eliminate or greatly reduce the huge overhang of the unemployed that depresses not only the wages of the employed workers but also threatens to displace the employed altogether.

All the labour relations laws under the sun will not protect the job security of employed workers. The growth of casualisation is one of the symptoms of job insecurity. Rising unemployment, as a result of increasing de-industrialisation, is another. The only thing that will guarantee job security for blue-collar workers is the fundamental restructuring of South Africa's industries in which unchecked privileges and patronage are taken from existing industries, and emergent industries are allowed to flourish. In short, if we continue to be what we are and do what we do then our outcomes will remain what they are and our prospects will continue to worsen.

The underclass as voting fodder

The first thing that distinguishes South Africa from the rest of the African continent is that it has no peasantry. The British destroyed peasant agriculture and peasant households at the end of the 19th century in order to create a working class for the mining industry. However, the partial industrialisation of South Africa did not lead to the creation of a modern

43

working class, as happened in the United States. Rather, it created a massive underclass that has not been absorbed into the production system.

This underclass today forms the largest voting bloc in South Africa's electoral system. It is the mainstay of ANC voters, accounting for nearly 70% of the people who vote for the ANC. The underclass gets rewarded economically in various ways through a number of welfare programmes. This expenditure constitutes a transfer of resources from production to consumption, and is one of the major contributors to our stunted capitalist society.

Civil society: Independent professionals, non-profit organisations and new entrepreneurs

A part of South Africa's urban population is made up of a diversity of highly skilled people and independent operators who provide numerous services that range from healthcare to engineering services, media to film, television and musical productions and religious services. All these activities are carried out through small and medium-sized enterprises.

Some of these enterprises operate for profit but many others are not-for-profit organisations. This sector provides South African society with a unique sense of dynamism and creativity. We exclude civil society in much of our analysis

44

as to date it has emerged as heterogeneous and disorganised and so has played an unsystematic and marginal role in South African society as we understand it today. As such, it has failed to influence any particular grouping to any significant degree.

A shifting interaction

We now address how to understand the present problem facing South African society in the context of history and the social structure presented above. Since each group has particular, stated objectives, then we would expect that these constitute a motivation for behaviour. These stated objectives are not entirely exhaustive of what these groups seek to achieve but they do illustrate the inherent conflict of interest between objectives; it is not possible to achieve some without compromising others, at least not simultaneously. And this is at the heart of the conflict in this society.

Below we have converted the social structure of South Africa into a series of diagrams illustrating combinations of how differing groups have interacted historically as well as in the current environment. The emergence of a traditionally antagonistic relationship between capital and labour and the current uncertainty surrounding the prospective nature of any interaction between any of the groups can be explained through the role of the state in the development of the country, and how the state then interacts with capital, labour, the elite and the unemployed.

British colonialism and Afrikaner nationalism

Figure 2.4, on the facing page, can be applied both to the period of British colonialism as well as Afrikaner nationalism though specific details may differ. During these times, capital, the state and the elite had a common, interdependent synergistic association, which was cooperative and stable. The relationship between the state and formal labour and between the state and the unemployed was characteristically authoritarian; it was reinforced by violence and it was unstable. Capital had an indirect relationship with both the unemployed and informal labour as well as formal labour. This relationship was always mediated by the state. Recruitment was involuntary and by fiat such that there was neither a requisite to compete for resources or to pay competitively for these. Production was sustained to the extent that capital could perform its traditional role of organising it and to some extent funding it, largely assisted by the state, which provided targeted and sustained financing as well as directing a steady and cheap mass of labour for whatever purpose capital demanded.

46

Figure 2.4 **Interaction during British colonialism and Afrikaner nationalism**

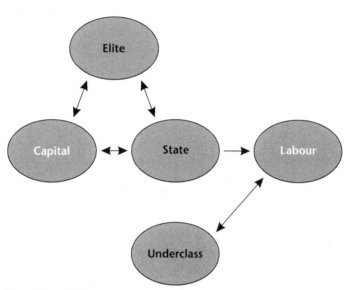

Source: Nobantu Mbeki.

In this environment, capital was able to sustain all manner of productive activity consistent with industrialisation in a fully protected environment, with neither a requisite for efficiency nor risk taking. In each of these eras the state benefited in its ability to reproduce consistently and with little compromise. Under colonialism, when formal labour was not militant and the unemployed were heavily restricted and isolated both spatially as well as ideologically, given their

47

subsistence existence and the onerous fiscal dues imposed upon them, the system was able to function. The crisis came in characteristic stagnation; the economic machine, in being protected and inefficient, became an unsustainable drain on state resources and society at large because it required sustained violence to function.

The era of Afrikaner nationalism repeated and reinforced the British colonialism structure, but two things changed. First, industrialisation led to a concentration of formal labour in urban areas, with the unintended consequence that labour was able to be more organised and so increasingly militant. The result was that the state had to divert resources at an accelerating rate toward the suppression of unrest and the maintenance of order and less toward sustaining the production machine. Second, this escalation of violence was consistent with a rebalancing of power. It allowed for the emergence of a countervailing force to the previously unrestricted and unimpeded reach of the state machinery, with the further unintended outcome that it weakened the association between the elite, capital and the state, the latter of which was no longer capable of systematically subsidising the others' functions, in the process further depressing these for all other groups.

African nationalism

As Figure 2.5 illustrates, post-1994 the state and labour can be said to have coalesced as the new controllers of the state and organised labour had been partners of the anti-apartheid. More importantly, the state has become functionally indistinct from labour so that reasonable expectations are that the state will most likely act primarily in favour of labour before all other interests. This has led to interaction between *all* groups becoming unstable because no credible bilateral agreements can be established between groups as a consequence.

Figure 2.5 **Interaction during transition to African nationalism**

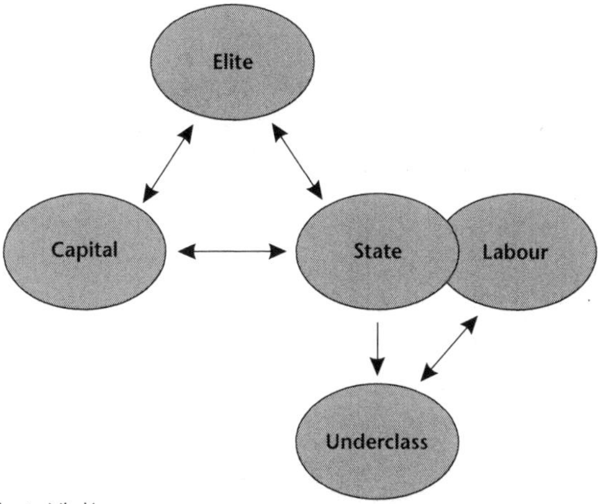

Source: Nobantu Mbeki.

Capital created a new type of elite through Black Economic Empowerment as a planning requisite, in response to the threat of labour militancy at best and nationalisation at worst. An increasingly powerless state and organised labour have scrambled to lap up what crumbs have been left, joining the rent-seeking behaviour of the elite while continuing to legitimise the perverse state of affairs. The inability of any group, including the state itself, to wrestle authority over events directly results from the origins and constitution of the current elite.

While in Figure 2.4, the elite, constituting owners of capital themselves, maintained an autonomous existence from all other groups – and more importantly reinforced a common goal – under African nationalism this is no longer the case. The new elite have become middlemen, emerging in part as a consequence of a trade between owners of capital and members of the previous government and has been augmented by the current state.

This new elite has no existence independent of the state or capital. They own nothing and have no productive capacity. But in the absence of transparency with the management of state revenues, it has access and influence when and where it matters. Since the elite has no existence independent of these groups, it forces tradeoffs between itself and the constituent groups. Because of this middleman role, negotiations are conducted in dark spaces, and the result renders state institutions even more opaque and susceptible to extortion both by the elite and capital. But this new elite has emerged as a double-edged sword for capital; its members are able to obstruct the ends of both the state and capital as they serve two masters, allowing them to extort both. Neither the state nor capital could have envisaged that the sustenance of the elite would become this costly this quickly, threatening political support for the current administration and stagnating capital's dissolution of South African exposure or their ability to salvage what's left.

The situation we find ourselves in today

Today both the state and capital find themselves at an impasse. Capital unwittingly dissolved its direct means of interacting with government in trying to establish, through BEE, a bulwark between itself and organised labour. Interaction between capital and the state is mediated by the elite, which by its very character can extort a toll for even the most basic and routine services. Disintermediation has proven costly and ineffective, with no guarantee that the elite will systematically pursue any one bloc's end. Capital cannot take anything as a given and so cannot plan, and consequently increasingly does not engage in

51

any behaviour that requires a long-term commitment. Any long-term planning is precluded because it is prohibitively costly since it is impossible to predict any course of action since any series of actions is subject to being interrupted at any stage in the process. More importantly, this new elite has caused a convergence not in objectives but rather in means of achieving given ends, namely corruption. Their existence presents a source of intractable instability that has accelerated a fracturing of society both because the elite are unpredictable and act haphazardly and operate without circumscription. (This point is discussed in greater detail in Chapter 4.)

Figure 2.6 **Present interaction**

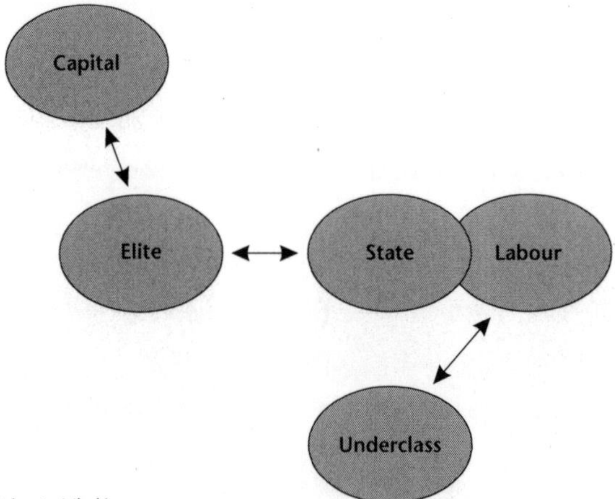

Source: Nobantu Mbeki.

In Figure 2.6, it is clear how the groups have realigned. Capital has realigned to only interact with the elite, with no direct interaction with the state. This is one of the main causes of instability in South Africa – it is not possible to legislate and enforce agreements between capital and the elite, only between capital and the state. The elite then manages the relationship with the state and labour, which have merged, leaving them together to interact with the underclass.

Capital has long lost its monopoly on the exploitation of state resources to achieve its own private objectives. Without recourse to violence as a means of suppression as previous state apparatuses had, the new administration has had to juggle a series of mutually exclusive outcomes. Each group acted independently and in a conflicting manner, with no incentive to do otherwise, whereas the state either legislated to achieve particular outcomes or attempted to persuade all groups toward a common goal. Legislation has not worked well both because monitoring has not been particularly effective and enforcement has been arbitrary, leaving an incentive to circumvent rules and conventions since, for all intents and purposes, it is possible to get away with it.

Capital has lost control of the state, and the state has, at best, a tenuous hold over all other groups. Consequently, the current administration has been presented with, and is unable to diffuse, what is essentially a ticking time bomb.

The present set of circumstances has a similar character to previous ones in times of periodic crisis: stagnation and then the onset of instability. Currently the unemployed seek income but this does not arise from traditional sources such as peasant agriculture. The unemployed, being the current administration's primary constituency, receive some sustenance from the acceleration in income redistribution through government transfers. That this income has not occurred through the net creation of work is what makes it unsustainable, as seen in the high and rising proportion of fiscal expenditure as well as escalating fiscal borrowing. Tactically, the mistake government has made is to widen the net rather than focus on the quality of these interventions because what they require is a quantum, namely as many people as possible voting favourably.

For as long as the legitimacy of the state remains at issue due to the opaque nature of the relationship between capital, the state and the elite, the ruling party will attempt to compensate by trying to buy the votes of the underclass and the unemployed at an accelerating rate. This approximates the historical diversion of state resources at an accelerating rate away from other production capability building functions, which has signalled systemic decline in previous periods of crisis and change.

The consistent eruption of localised conflict of increasing

severity and scale signals the obsolescence of the current order. The state is failing to resolve conflicts; it is no longer an independent mediator as it has partnerships with labour and covert relationships with capital that are mediated by the elite.

That this is becoming endemic signals the end of an era that will be characterised by the death of its institutions, a failure to cope with particular emergent *types* of problems. In this instance, the system is failing to cope with particular types of social unrest relating to the isolated, unemployed and poor, including violent protest, violent personal crimes, violent expressions of xenophobia, violent service delivery protests and increasingly violent responses of political dissent. In contrast to vocal and widely documented criticism by the middle class and civil society, it is rather this – the violence from the unemployed and poor – that has signalled to the rest of the society that they can evade legislation and get away with it since it is only violence that has visibly swayed the authorities. The dissatisfaction with general government performance is finding expression in campaigns on a national scale and movements around fairly localised issues that become focal points for disgruntlement, such as the introduction of e-tolling in Gauteng, which has sprouted a civil disobedience campaign. Both non-adherence to rules and violence are escalating and neither the legal nor social institutions can arrest this trend.

The state faces an impasse. The use of violence by the state to enforce legal arrangements by definition precludes acceptance of its legitimacy. This signals more than indecision; it signals a state that is overwhelmed, which has become paralytic in the face of circumstance and which, in turn, precipitates further non-adherence. In short, the obsolescence of the current order is unfolding as a violent and anarchic tendency. The sheer scale of the problem of enforcing order has exploded since fires now erupt on all sides. This is reflected in the fiscus; spending on enforcing law and order has increased costs of militarised policing, expanding the capacity of penal institutions, and so the list continues to the exclusion of other functions.

Resources are again being diverted at an increasing rate to secure control over the mass unemployed for exactly the same reasons as in other periods in this country's history. There is, however, an important qualitative difference to how this is unfolding.

In this instance, individuals are themselves privately incurring the cost of providing exclusive functions traditionally performed by the state, which further undermines the authority of the state whose functions are increasingly privatised. Since these are privately owned and operated, individuals are not accountable to public institutions in how they behave. This has led to a creation of what are essentially multiple mini-fiefdoms governed by their own rules with the same flavour as fractured, failed states governed by warlords. So there is a widening area (in both physical span and legislative scope) that is beyond the mediation of the state. It is only a matter of time before individual interests and spheres of influence themselves come to overlap and conflict; a confrontation that cannot be resolved by public institutions.

In order to restore the legitimacy of the state in South Africa, we have to recreate a productive economic model. To do that, the tenure of capital has to be restored, which means the elite, as shown on Figure 2.6, cannot retain its position as an intermediary between capital and the state. Capital has to have a direct, unmediated relationship with the state. Similarly, there has to be a direct relationship between the underclass, the state and capital. This is the only way to ensure a growing economy. The current model actually reinforces a parasitic elite that is living off both capital and the state. Such a relationship does not lead to increased investment but to growing consumption.

CHAPTER 3

THE HISTORICAL CONTEXT OF SOUTH AFRICA

South Africa is one of a number of countries founded outside Europe by European powers during the 16th and 17th centuries. These countries had a number of common features:

❏ They were founded on the export of population and technology from Western Europe.
❏ They were founded on genocide against indigenous peoples.

❏ They imported slaves from Africa and/or Asia.

❏ They exploited the natural resources and labour of the new territories for benefit of old countries.

❏ Their politico-economic systems were designed by the European colonising powers.

❏ They were established through the destruction of the technical skills of indigenous peoples, where the latter survived.

The countries that met the above description were mostly in the Americas. Most of South America became a colony of Spain and Portugal, while North America and some of the Caribbean islands became British, French and Spanish colonies.

In Africa only two countries fell under this classification: South Africa and Mauritius. Although the latter did not have an indigenous population, it had all the other attributes.

South Africa had a great deal in common with the former slave-owning countries of the Caribbean, but especially with the United States. Both South Africa and the United States were British colonies and their economies fuelled the economic development of Britain. While the United States provided cotton, which formed the backbone of the Industrial Revolution, the discovery of diamonds and gold in South Africa 150 years ago has been a source of enormous profits, which have continued to flow into the British economy.

At the end of the American Revolutionary War with Britain in 1783, the northern region of the United States spent most of the next 80 years in a struggle to achieve economic independence. The central objective of their economic independence was to enable entrepreneurs to gain access to British industrial and scientific knowledge so they could establish new enterprises, including the cotton textile factories that constituted the foundation of the Industrial Revolution.

The British government wanted none of that. In its view, the role of their colony was to be a supplier of raw cotton lint to British textile factories as well as a protected market for British manufactured goods. As Michael Lind points out in *Land of Promise: An Economic History of the United States*, the British went to great lengths to frustrate American entrepreneurs from acquiring British technological expertise, going so far as to prohibit the emigration to the United States of artisans and technicians who had been trained in the textile industries.

In its effort to frustrate the new country's industrialisation, the British had the backing of the slave owners in the South who grew cotton for export. They did not want to jeopardise their main export market by upsetting the British through stealing their textile-manufacturing technology.

61

The tussle between the North and South and Britain culminated in the American Civil War of 1861–65. The defeat of the South eventually destroyed the political and economic hold Britain had over the United States. Industrialisation of the country took off after that, with its entrepreneurs building iron and steel, engineering, oil and gas, finance, electric, textile and eventually motor-vehicle industries.

This abbreviated story of economic development in the United States helps us to answer why it has become one of the richest and most productive countries in the world while South Africa has been mired at the bottom of the middle-income trap, with half of its adult population locked outside a productive role in the formal economy. The Americans overcame the obstacles put in their way by history by creating a genuine capitalist society.

South Africa, by contrast, has so far only partially met those challenges, leaving it as a stunted capitalist society.

Of course, South Africa is different from the United States in that a large part of the indigenous population survived. However, the indigenous people lost all the assets they previously possessed, particularly land and livestock, but most importantly they lost their traditional technical skills.

Two things are therefore important to understand about the formation of South Africa. The first is that for the last 150 years the indigenous population was effectively prohibited from acquiring Western technical and managerial skills, which might have replaced the traditional technical skills they had lost, and they were denied the ability to acquire modern business and industrial assets. The second is that the population brought from Europe by the Dutch East India Company in the 17th and 18th centuries became increasingly isolated from modern Europe and therefore did not have the skills that European populations developed during those critical two centuries, which culminated in the Industrial Revolution. Most manual work was done by the slaves, which further contributed to the loss of skills amongst whites.

The de-skilling of South Africa's population, black and white, had hugely adverse consequences on the country's future economic development. When minerals were discovered, the population did not have the scientific, technical, financial and managerial wherewithal to start and develop the all-important mining industry. The development of the industry was thus undertaken by the foreign immigrants who flooded into South Africa from the 1860s through to the end of the 19th century.

This immigration wave brought people from the United Kingdom, the United States, Australia and parts of Europe. They brought their own technical skills and managerial systems that created the migrant labour structure for exploiting black labour which continues to this day. They also brought new industries to sustain the new population and supply their more refined lifestyles, in comparison with local white and black inhabitants.

Those leading the companies that eventually controlled the mining industry in South Africa were representatives of London investors. These mining magnates, in cahoots with the British government, eventually took military control of South Africa in 1901. Between 1902 and 1910, when they handed political power to Afrikaner nationalists, the British reorganised South African society and the state so the country would continue to supply minerals and profits to Britain long after they had direct political control.

The aristocracy from which the leadership of the indigenous peoples came was decimated during the long, drawn-out process of military conquest. At the end of it African communities were in a state of shock; they did not know who to turn to as many members of the aristocracies who survived the wars of resistance started collaborating with the European victors.

In this period of bewilderment, two groups emerged that were sympathetic to the defeated communities. One was the European missionaries, especially the London Missionary Society who had been critical of the oppressive and exploitative policies towards the indigenous people and the colonists. The second were the mission-educated African groups that started to articulate public opinion of their new class.

The formation of the black elite

From the middle of the 19th century, a new class of African and coloured mission school-educated individuals started to emerge. This group soon became sufficiently established as a propertied class to start founding African-language newspapers, and thus participating in the politics of the Cape and Natal colonies.

Among the former slaves, imams played a similar leadership role, while passage Indians – the merchants and professionals – provided similar leadership amongst Indian indentured workers.

In 1884, *Imvo Zabantsundu* was founded by John Tengo Jabavu and *Ilanga Lase Natal* was founded by John Dube in 1904. Other newspapers established during the same period were Sol Plaatje's *Koranta ea Becoana* and Mahatma Gandhi's *Indian Opinion*.

In his unpublished MA thesis, 'The African Middle Class in South Africa 1884–1964', Moeletsi found that in 1904 Natal had 150 missionary schools attended by 11 000 pupils, while in the same year the Cape had 60 000 African pupils taught by 200 teachers. By the end of the 19th century, Africans in Natal (excluding Zululand) owned 68 000 acres in freehold; 34 000 acres in quitrent (long leases); while 217 000 acres of Crown lands had been sold to Africans, under long terms of payment similar to European purchasers.

Meanwhile, Fort Hare University, an initiative pioneered by Walter Rubusana, a member of the Cape parliament, was built with contributions by Africans and opened its doors in 1916.

But the most important undertaking by the African bourgeoisie at the time was the founding of various important black political parties, including the Natal Indian Congress, founded in 1894, and the African People's Organisation, founded in 1904, followed by the African National Congress in 1912.

In these struggles of nearly a century and a half, the black working class and the black masses in general played a supportive role. They did not set the agenda. The agenda of black nationalism was set by the black elite that inherited the leadership mantle from the defeated African aristocracy, and the black working class followed.

Through the 1900s, the black elite guarded its leadership position so jealously that in the 1940s it established the ANC Youth League to ensure that the leadership of the black working class did not fall into the hands of communists. This was the main argument that persuaded then ANC president

Dr AB Xuma to approve the establishment of the ANC Youth League in 1944.

In its founding documents the Youth League wrote:

> The African people in South Africa are oppressed as a group with a particular colour. They suffer national oppression in common with thousands and millions of oppressed colonial peoples in other parts of the world. African nationalism is the dynamic national liberatory creed of the oppressed people ... Africans must build a powerful liberation movement, and in order that the National movement should have inner strength and solidarity it should adopt the National liberators creed – African nationalism, and it should be led by Africans themselves.

Nelson Mandela, never one to mince his words, wrote:

> There are certain groups which seek to impose on our struggle cut and dried formulae, which so far from clarifying the issues only serve to obscure the fundamental issue that we are oppressed not as a class, but as a people, as a nation. Such wholesale importation of methods and tactics which might have succeeded in other countries, like Europe, where conditions are different, might harm the cause of our people's freedom, unless we are quick in building a militant mass liberation movement.

And the journal of the Transvaal Youth League, *African Lodestar*, contained this commentary in 1950:

> Since the workers in the country are oppressed primarily because they are Africans and only secondarily because they are workers, it is clear that the exotic plant of Communism cannot flourish on African soil; this plant will not take kindly to the soil thus it is bound to wither and die out. If it remains it is likely to ruin the soil without any benefit to itself as it is now happening.

The establishment of the Youth League proved a success in that it marginalised the Communist Party, which had started to make headway among the urban black masses in the 1940s, after the Soviet Union joined the war against the Nazis in 1941. After the Second World War's national liberation struggles, the communists as well as the working class played a followership role.

Later, the communists would go even further and become the praise singers of African nationalism, for which they were permitted to be an authorised lobby.

While the African nationalists were able to subdue their communist opponents, they failed to prevail over their more powerful adversaries – the mining magnates, white workers and Afrikaner nationalists. Eventually African nationalists had to settle for a compromise that preserved intact the economic and social interests of their main adversaries in return for universal franchise and a multiparty constitutional democracy.

Not surprisingly, the African elite came out of the negotiations for democracy with very little. Their main achievement was the right to manage the state and to live off government revenues. They could not, however, change South Africa's economic model.

South Africa's periods of production

Since its establishment in 1652, South African capitalism has gone through five distinct periods of production: the Dutch East India Company period; two British periods; the Afrikaner nationalist period; and now the African nationalist period. Each period has been driven by its own dominant political elite, which has served the elite's economic, political and social objectives.

The Dutch East India Company's objective was to create a halfway station that would supply its ships with fresh foods. The Dutch therefore brought new crops to South Africa, especially wheat and grapes, as well as new workers – slaves – to grow the crops. They also brought several technologies and inventions, such as the wheel, the horse, guns and textiles that did not exist in South Africa at the time. The Dutch system, which lasted until the British took over in 1795, was a production-driven system par excellence. It was very cruel to its workers and was founded on the genocide of the San and Khoi, the indigenous peoples of the Western Cape.

The British continued with the Dutch system until 1834, when they abolished slavery. From the 1830s until the 1890s, the British developed an African peasant-based economy in the Eastern Cape, and later in Natal, by introducing freehold land ownership and the use of animal-drawn agricultural implements.

The discovery of diamonds and gold during the last quarter of the 19th century caused the British mining investors to turn against the peasant agriculture promotion system, demanding it be dismantled in order to release African males from peasant agriculture to go and work in the mines. The most outspoken advocate for the abandonment of peasant agriculture was Cecil John Rhodes, founder of De Beers Consolidated Mines and one-time prime minister of the Cape Colony. During his tenure as prime minister he promulgated the Glen Grey Act of 1894, which imposed taxes on African men in territories under British control in order to force African men to earn cash by working in the mines.

These measures led to the creation of the second British

production system, which would come to be known as the Minerals-Energy Complex (MEC). The MEC was built on the ruins of South Africa's collapsed peasant agriculture, and continues to be driven by African migrant labour and is significantly funded by stakeholders based in London.

The Afrikaner nationalists, during the 84 years they controlled the state from 1910 to 1994, refined the British system.

The Afrikaner elite who controlled the Orange Free State and the Transvaal expropriated land from the indigenous peoples during several wars in the second half of the 19th century. Essentially pastoralists, they only started to build a modern agricultural system after the British handed them the South African state in 1910.

One of the first actions of the government of Louis Botha, himself a landowner from Natal, was the creation of the Land Bank, in order to provide cheap credit to commercial farmers.

This system went on to mobilise and organise cheap black labour and to establish a cheap, effective and extensive transport and communication infrastructure to serve commercial farmers. In the process, other infrastructure-related industries were established, such as iron and steel, fertilisers, oil from coal and armaments. Lastly, they developed an extensive education system to train farmers, their children

71

and their managers in agricultural and veterinary sciences and other skills in food marketing, processing and storage.

The driving motive behind all these developments was to enrich commercial farmers so they could supply the growing industrial and mining towns sprouting up across the country, as well as export to British and other world markets, which would enable South Africa to buy the technology it needed to grow agriculture and other industries.

In the many analyses of South Africa's 360 years of capitalism, focus has rightly been on the suffering inflicted on the black population in the process of building the production capabilities of the capitalist system. Today a new story is unfolding, however. That is the story of the dismantling of South Africa's production capacity. This time it is in the name of humanising South Africa's capitalism by transforming it from a production system into a consumption system.

British economic legacy

The intensive preoccupation with the National Party's apartheid policies has led many to believe that Afrikaner nationalists created South Africa's modern economy. But, as we have shown, it was the British who established the South African economy during the last quarter of the 19th century.

They did not just reorganise the economy, they created it from scratch to suit their purposes.

Figure 3.1 **South Africa's legacy from British rule: 1795–1910**

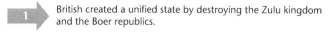
British created a unified state by destroying the Zulu kingdom and the Boer republics.

British created a mining industry linked to London for finance; this mining industry still accounts for most of South Africa's exports.

British destroyed African peasant agriculture and converted the rural population to generate permanent revolving male labour migrants and a pool of unemployed females.

British set the stage for competing nationalisms to fight it out over state revenues extracted from the cheap black labour system.

British created the southern African region initially for labour supply and later as one of the largest metal producers in the world.

Source: Moeletsi Mbeki.

In Frank Welsh's *A History of South Africa,* he writes that the British conquered the Cape Colony from the Dutch for strategic reasons: to control the Cape route to Asia and ensure it did not fall into enemy hands at the time of Napoleon's France. In the language of global strategists, the Cape is a 'choke point': the power that controls this point controls the right of passage for ships that have to transit through that route. Besides the Cape, there are two other

73

choke points around Africa: the entry into the Red Sea from the Indian Ocean, the Gulf of Aden, and the entry into the Mediterranean Sea from the Atlantic Ocean, the Strait of Gibraltar.

For the 75 years between 1795 and 1870, the Cape was only of geo-strategic value to the British. But the South African economy as we know it today was created by the British between the years of 1871 – when the diamond-mining town of Kimberley was proclaimed by British Colonial Secretary, Lord Kimberley – and 1886, when, as president of the South Africa Republic, Paul Kruger proclaimed the public gold diggings on several farms in what came to be known as the Witwatersrand. In the same year, the mining village of Johannesburg was proclaimed.

The Boers, who controlled what came to be known as the Transvaal in the 1880s when the Witwatersrand deposits were discovered, had neither the capital nor the expertise required to exploit the deposits. The deposits soon came under control of British companies and, before long, the South African Republic became the British colony of the Transvaal.

The story of how the British took ownership of South Africa's diamond and gold deposits and went on to create the Union of South Africa has been told too many times to require repeating here. What warrants repetition, though, are the economic legacies that the British left behind as these continue to influence if not determine outright South Africa's future.

For a period of almost 150 years since South Africa's vast mineral endowment of diamonds, gold, coal, platinum, etc., was uncovered from the 1870s onwards, the country has been one of the main drivers of British prosperity and scientific and managerial development. But South Africa's wealth did not just enrich British citizens; it enriched many people in Europe as well as North America. Giving an account of the different nationalities involved in digging for and trading in diamonds in 1871, as indicated by Charles Chapman in *A Voyage from Southampton to Cape Town, in the Union Company's Mail Steamer*, one traveller reported:

> There were faces of every conceivable cast and colour of the human race: the Kaffir, the Englishman, the Hottentot, and the Dutchman, the Fingo and the German, the Yankee and the Swede, the Frenchman and the Turk, the Norwegian and the natives, the Russian and the Greek – in fact a smattering of people from every nation on the face of the earth – digging, sifting, and sorting from morning till night, day after day, month after month, until they have obtained what they consider sufficient.

75

The vast mineral wealth that has been dug and carted out of South Africa over a century and a half is only one part of the story of the exploitation of the country's natural resources. What is often overlooked are the vast fortunes made by American and European suppliers of the technology and other know-how employed in South Africa's mining industries. This is an important part of the economic legacy the British left behind in South Africa: technological dependence.

From the very beginning, the South African mining industry not only depended on European and American financial resources that were largely channelled through London, it also depended on plants and machinery imported from the West. The processing of the metal out of the rock as well as the eventual refining was done largely with imported equipment.

The story did not end there. Over the years South African minerals have been the subjects of extensive industrial research on their uses, including platinum, of which 80% of global reserves are said to be in South Africa. Platinum is now used in jewellery, electronics, autocatalytic convertors, medicine, computers and weapon systems. In all these uses South Africa was, and is, the supplier of the raw material while the British and their close allies, especially the Americans, provided the intellectual and technical wherewithal. All this know-how comes at a cost to South Africa in the form of patents, copyrights and the equipment itself.

An even more glaring recent example is the case of chrome ore. South Africa is estimated to have most of the world deposits of this metal, which is a core input in the production of stainless steel. Today a large part of ferrochrome on the world market is produced out of China from imported South African chrome ore.

An April 2014 *Business Day* article noted that South Africa's ferrochrome industry shrunk from 51% of global market share in 2003 to 32%, while China's share – fuelled partly by exports of chrome ore from South Africa – rose to 37%. A spokesperson for Merafe Resources, a major chrome miner, told the paper that they had pushed the government to act for years 'on the export of unbeneficiated chrome ore but has now largely given up'. This must be a case of a bad habit acquired during the British era in the 19th and 20th centuries extending into the 21st century.

The single most important British economic legacy to South Africa, however, was not technical and financial issues in the mining sector. Given the political will, many of these issues could have been overcome and, on a limited scale, efforts were made to overcome this, including the development of the iron and steel industries in the late 1920s and early 1930s; the development of oil from coal after the Second World War; and the broader armaments industry after the 1970s.

The single most lasting British economic legacy to South Africa is, rather, how the massive, cheap supplies of African labour to the mines and related support industries, such as municipalities, infrastructure development and eventually agriculture, were orchestrated. The migrant labour system that resulted remains the backbone of the South African economy, though the mining companies today are exploring efforts to replace most migrant workers with machines. But even the introduction of greater mechanisation does not substantially change the callous migrant labour system inherited from the British. The system survives more or less intact to this day despite promises in the Mining Charter to abolish it.

At the heart of the migrant labour system is the ruthless exploitation of the labour of African mineworkers, most of whom originate from the rural areas and whose families are still living there. In the past their families were forbidden from living with them at their place of work by the pass system and limited duration contracts. Minor modifications introduced by unionisation, the Mining Charter and Freedom of Movement under the 1996 Constitution have, however, not changed the key elements of this hugely exploitative system.

According to Morley Nkosi, in his book *Mining Deep: The Origins of the Labour Structure in South Africa*:

The racially divided and hierarchical labour structure inherited from the copper mining industry in Namaqualand had become entrenched. And the factors which ensured its continuation were the consolidation of the diamond mines into larger operating units, their dependence on skilled white miners who supervised the large number of native labour, the state's intervention in generating the supply and control of native labour, and the institutionalisation of the contract-migrant labour system and its appendage, the compounds housing native labour.

An important aspect of the migrant labour system that is often overlooked is the devastation it brought to families in rural communities. In the 19th century the British introduced and encouraged African rural communities to use animal-drawn ploughs and other agricultural implements, which quickly replaced the indigenous hand-held hoe that was mainly used by women; with animal-drawn implements a farmer could cultivate more land.

In the Cape Blue Book of 1874, the magistrate of Middledrift in the Eastern Cape wrote: 'cultivation by the old hoe has been entirely super ceded by the plough, an indication of progress which gives me a great pleasure to report'.

With the discovery of minerals, the British reversed their agricultural policies for Africans. Using a multitude of taxes imposed on African rural households, males were compelled to abandon farming, and their families became increasingly dependent on remittances from male members working for wages in the mines.

The migrant labour system gave rise to a massive army of unemployed African females who were locked in rural areas by numerous legal and economic devices – a system that continues today. The planned mechanisation of the mines will only aggravate this situation as it will further offload unemployed African males back into the rural communities and into the shanty towns that ring South African cities. The low level of labour participation in the economy that is much lamented by the National Planning Commission is but the other side of the coin of the migrant labour system.

One hundred and fifty years of mining precious minerals has left the African people of South Africa with a legacy of massive unemployment, poverty and one of the worse disease loads in the world. Side by side with this vast ocean of misery are levels of opulence that are comparable to any Samuel Taylor Coleridge imagined existed in Xanadu.

CHAPTER 4

HOW CAPITAL IS COMPLICIT IN ECONOMIC STAGNATION

In order to understand the intractability of South African capital's negotiating position and how individual firms and industries undermine the very stability they require, we have taken an academic approach toward understanding this systemic problem. Our perspective is that the persistent erosion of stability arises from actions set by capital that set a particular framework. The way in which different industries behave amongst themselves arises because this way of interacting has become self-perpetuating, reproducing itself. Much of the emphasis in ongoing discourse has been on circumstantial conditions surrounding what are essentially the outcomes of this underlying process. This chapter seeks rather to explore the process in order to form the basis of a full and meaningful understanding of the prospects of this society.

The difference between volatility and stability

To lower volatility is not the same thing as to create stability. It is unfortunate that the terms volatile and unstable are used interchangeably in common usage. They are not – at least as far as planning is concerned.

Firms enter, operate and survive in volatile environments all the time. Volatility varies in degree and, as such, it can be adjusted for. It is only a matter of how much effort is required, and how much that effort costs.

Stability, however, either exists or it does not. When it doesn't exist it is impossible to plan, and when planning is impossible, there is no way to rule out catastrophe; there is no way to determine whether to apply resources because there is no way of ensuring that these are not being poured into a void. Money is spent and it may be wiped out tomorrow with no chance of recovering it.

With instability, the environment elementally transforms into one in which prior decisions and plans no longer make sense. This gives rise to a basic impetus to want to generate and maintain stability because large-scale environments are only fully recoverable over a long horizon. So whenever any changes occur that undermine stability, it is a very clear signal not to make more commitments.

The unitary cause of depressed investment is the realisation that South Africa has lost the ability to generate and reproduce stability. Specific ruptures in the course of growth and development have all coincided and the environment has qualitatively and fundamentally changed. This becomes important since, if any intervention to change present circumstances is sought, then it needs to resolve the basic cause – the system itself.

The role of capital

In the context of our argument about stability, there are two important features to understand about the role that capital plays in the economy. The first is how firms interact with their environment and the rest of society. The second is how the prior behaviour of firms can be interpreted as having systematically caused the conditions that undermine stability today.

83

So why has capital in South Africa made particular choices and what have been the consequences? Our emphasis is on the behaviour of large firms in the context of their own plans and we seem to ignore significant external developments. This does not mean that key changes in legislation or the regulatory environment are peripheral, parallel or unrelated, but rather the concern here is with how firms had a hand in bringing them about.

Capital seeks to actively influence its external environment and this impinges on broader society in a very different way than is normally conceived. There is no reason to assume that the stability firms require, and what they do to bring it about, is optimal for the rest of society. It also means that in particular instances firms will actively intervene in their environment beyond the scope of their traditionally conceived operational sphere to bring about particular conditions. It is the wide span of activity within the firm's external environment with which we are concerned. Firms are complex, their behaviour is complex, their environment is complex, that is a given. Ensuring that stability reproduces in the environment is a significant component of large firms' planning procedures. This means that stability is not a means to an end. It is the end. All other objectives are intermediate.

Overlapping industries

Why would firms of different characteristics and at different stages of development, with competing objectives and possibly conflicting objectives, simultaneously seek stability, especially since its achievement would have a differentiated impact on them? Why and how would they act collectively to bring about communal stability? And why would individual firms, which nevertheless are oligopolistic and interdependent, and in many cases collusive, also be collectively considered as a single entity?

South Africa has industrialised largely on the basis of domestic capital.[1] To the extent that South African firms are multinational, they are part of a class of emerging-market multinational firms, but differ from their counterparts in that they do not remain based in the markets from which they originate.[2] The 'centre of strategic decision-making'[3] shifts to external and critically mature markets. This means South African multinationals raise capital and operate in and grow through acquisitions from foreign markets. They expand abroad while only maintaining market presence to the extent that they still retain market dominance.

So why does this happen? Why would firms with more or less uncontested power systematically scale down presence in a sphere they not only dominate and would be able to dominate indefinitely? What is so bleak about that prospective future?

Figure 4.1 shows three overlapping firms contained within an industry, and then within the economy and society. Note the area of overlap between Firm A and Firm B and Firm A and Firm C. These are areas of cost overlap between firms. Already the precondition for stability to emerge is evident; firms must have similar cost structures or the cost dispersion between firms must be low.[4]

A specific feature of South African firms, particularly under the strategic objective of Afrikaner nationalism, was sufficient to produce this result.[5] These firms were highly interlocking in virtue of the specificity of the developmental

Figure 4.1 **The prerequisites for stability**

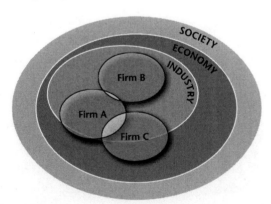

Source: Nobantu Mbeki.

plan and later in virtue of 'independent' cross ownership that was sufficient to produce this effect even if they had highly dispersed costs and engaged in dissimilar activities.

Firms A, B and C will make independent decisions in areas that do not overlap with those of other firms. Where overlapping occurs, bilateral or multilateral decisions are made. The higher the degree of collective similarity, the less costly it is to enforce and maintain agreements between firms. With mutual inconsistency and so a high degree of conflict, which happens when firms enter and exit industries, conditions in industries become unstable at least until such a time as these areas of overlap can be reconstituted. The high degree of concentration in South African industry already tells such as story and the story is consistent with traditional approaches to industrial organisation. However, this suggests a further feature that remains under-explored.

Once constituted, areas of overlap mean there is a basic tendency for firms to evolve in a common way, permitting firms to economise. So when firms evolve in a similar way, it is because there are some strategic decisions that are no longer determined or managed independently. That is, firms eventually interlock if there is overlap. Notably, this is also why we use firms and capital interchangeably. When this happens individual firms will begin to act collectively and will tend to collude on anything that falls within the ambit of the group. This is because over time the group becomes intractable, or at the very least can only be undone at a significantly high cost. The planning requisite increases when firms interlock and so begin to evolve on a common, mutual path, and it rises even further when firms interlock with society at large. So stability is both a cause and consequence of planning. This is the internal reason why stability both exists and is actively sought. Firms' actions go from simply being interdependent to being collective, making collective decisions as an entity: capital. It is not simply the case that they choose to act unilaterally.

We immediately know that blocks of capital are competing to displace and/or dominate one another. That is, there is nevertheless an underlying rivalrous process of competition within which dominance is contested and must be asserted. It is not naturally occurring that firms come to act collectively. However, once they do, then it is a whole different matter; it becomes a sustained tendency to act collectively.

So the intervention that Afrikaner nationalism made, deliberate or otherwise, was to eliminate the first requisite in the lifecycle of firms. Even forms of integration were by conscious design. Then, more importantly, came collective purpose. It did not need to develop naturally between firms through trust, feasibility, trial and error and dominance. It was directly imposed in virtue of how the diversification of Afrikaner capital arose. So if there is overlap between the state and firms, and these interlock, then they will also evolve jointly from that point on.

However, we now already know an outcome of stability: in order for fundamental change to occur, an interlocking system cannot be modified by only changing some of its parts. All of its components must be modified more or less simultaneously, or it must be vacated in its entirety. We also know another feature; the same form of relationship exists between the state and corporate South Africa today – hence the systematic reproduction and role of the elite, which is the other counterpart of the gridlock on economic expansion.

Capital and the elites

The life of capital has extended beyond that of its political elites; a significant proportion of dominant firms have been around for a very, very long time. However, once capital and its elites interconnect, they also interlock. When elites change, this interrupts the entire process, requiring fresh plans; different players, a different regime, different set of 'anti-rules' emerge, as do different forms of interaction – all of which are costly, and in an unspecifiable way.

History has taught firms that elites change and cannot be relied on to keep themselves in a job, so the relationship between dominant capital and elites is symbiotic as much as it cannot be left to the short-lived successes of elites. Capital will try as far as possible to bring into the scope of direct control the requisites for stability. Hence the seemingly unwieldy span of firms' interests.

But the more interlinkages built into a system, the more inherently unstable it becomes.[6] Here then lies the limit of firms' power and control. This is explained in part by the process by which firms breach the industry boundary in Figure 4.1; in essence, firms bring costs of strategic importance that lie externally into the ambit of the everyday cost of doing business since it allows them to regularise these costs. An impetus for this arises externally in the following manner.

Stability within the boundaries of capital cannot exist in the absence of external stability. This stability is a prerequisite if new investment has to be undertaken. However, there are problems. The indirect and less assured nature of the relationship with the state specifically, and with society at large, is exacerbated by the indirect relationship that firms have with labour since this is itself of strategic importance in constituting the most autonomous members of society. Previously, organised labour by virtue of a direct correspondence to the state through the Tripartite Alliance was, in principle, capable of autonomous action. Now, the urban poor are capable of autonomous action independently of any other constituency in broad society even though an indirect association exists with the state.

As the state continues to fail to do its part, costs continue to ratchet in a completely unpredictable way. So the very eventuality capital expended significant cost to avoid is happening in spite of those costs having been incurred, and bring with them even more costs that cannot be quantified with any accuracy. The more this happens, the higher the impetus for firms to increase the span of their control on the society and hence the self-reinforcing and accelerating tendency towards stagnation and periodic crises.

In Figure 4.1, industry is only a component of society. The areas outside industry are essentially areas that are contestable and will be contested if they begin to interrupt internal processes. They are areas in which the collective actions in specific interlocking domains can conflict with those in other interlocking domains. Since these are not in the area that firms directly control, then firms do not dominate these. However, when the rest of society does not interlock, and so does not broadly evolve commonly, firms require additional, separate and possibly conflicting arrangements with different groups in order to maintain stability. Again, this means there

91

is a sense in which the manipulation of public institutions is efficient and necessary. So the scale of the required response by capital is rising as the scope of strategic pricing increases. And it is not just that these costs are unpredictable – they are implicitly too high.

Employment then has to decrease because profitability has declined. High persistent unemployment and inconsistent state behaviour then amplify and accelerate the effect. All this feeds back through the same process in an accelerating race to the bottom.

Planning, autonomy and stability

The problem then is that planning, autonomy and stability are a trifecta as shown in Figure 4.2. As such, there is a certain incoherence in communal planning. At issue is autonomy. It is a Catch-22 for this society.

In the context of our history, autonomy is necessary but undesirable since precedent has demonstrated that it is not always used in the public interest; rather, it is used to the detriment of public interest and with damaging consequences. However, where there exist rights, there must necessarily exist responsibilities. These, however, are largely divorced from each other in this society and/or are the subject of much abuse; it is also used as a means of extortion. However,

Figure 4.2 **The magic trifecta**

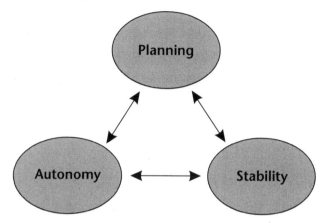

Source: Nobantu Mbeki.

it is unclear how these can exist separately in a society with private property and wherein rights are conferred in virtue of ownership.

Success and progress abound and are sustained where planning, autonomy and stability are simultaneously and continuously reconstituted. This is described as a problem for three reasons.

First, they are interdependent, but it is not clear that they can be sequenced. However, it is not possible to pursue one without simultaneously ensuring the presence of the others; nor is it possible to have one without the others. Second, to achieve any one of these alone is extremely difficult; none emerges spontaneously and is the outcome of sustained deliberate action. Third, because they are the outcome of intentionality, and while autonomy is a requisite, it potentially persistently undermines collective planning and collective stability. This is because autonomy is largely a prerogative. It is also because in being exclusive in intent and possession, autonomy inherently causes conflicts of interest that are not necessarily self-resolving. Neither will these necessarily regulate collective decisions, actions, motivations or outcomes, particularly if these must be more broadly inclusive. Knowing this immediately tells us that we can understand many features of the current situation simply by knowing that planning, autonomy and stability are inextricable.

Lack of investment

The South African market is highly concentrated,[7] and its firms have significant power. Within this, the preference is for firms to fund investment internally rather than in open market operations.[8] Interestingly, the 2013 Organisation for Economic Co-operation and Development report on South Africa observes in passing the 'de-coupling of the gross operating surplus and investment'. If firms typically would fund investment out of retained earnings precisely because it permits autonomy and meets planning requisites, why would they cease to do so?

Large-scale industry, such as mining and agriculture, is de-industrialising. For the most part, these firms grow investment at a rate comparable to depreciation, if at all. As a consequence, they have come to occupy a smaller share of productive capacity over time. Where net investment is positive, it is on a significantly smaller scale. This means that where accumulation is occurring, it cannot offset the loss in capacity from the shrinking proportion that traditional, large-scale industry occupies.

The preference for internal financing for investment directly relates to autonomy. The planning firm that proximately wants to grow at a particular rate may not immediately seek high profits.[9] It can also sustain itself for protracted periods without these. But it cannot indefinitely do so when profitability falls. The large firm that intends to a make profit in order to pay for investment will not invest in the absence of prior profit having been generated.[10] Strategies that allow large firms to reproduce themselves are unsuccessful because retained earnings deteriorated where they did not fail outright. That is, the 'financial crisis' was an anomaly as an impetus and simply the last in a series of things spanning decades that affected the profitability of South African firms. It is the only thing

95

that happened after a protracted period in South Africa's modern history that was incidental. It interrupted what we will term a brief 'golden period' in a post-independent South Africa.

From the perspective of firms, there are essentially two broad types of financing available for investment: internal financing and external financing. And if we broadly simplify further, the external funds available are borrowing (credit extension) and the internal funds are retained profits (broadly encapsulated in the operating surplus). Despite cyclical fluctuations, the shares of both have been broadly stable for decades, with external financing constituting over a third of all financing. The lion's share then has been retained earnings; it can then be said that there was actually a 'golden age' between the late 1990s and late 2000s in which profit and investment became aligned.

Without understating the role that external factors such as global deflation, persistently high commodity prices, high external demand for exports, and so on, played in this, it can be fairly said that this period also coincides with the tenure of our previous administration. The question, then, is how do we adjudicate the cause? That is, how much of this can we actually attribute to internal developments and how much is actually due to the windfall provided by external developments?

96

It is not so much the level or direction of costs – that is, it is not that inputs were lower and generally declining (and in some cases they were) – as much as they were fundamentally less volatile but also the environment less variant. Critically, this period, which incidentally was the longest sustained upswing in the business cycle since the Second World War, was one of unprecedented, sustained, ubiquitous and general stability. It is also a period in which capacity utilisation remained comparable to any other period despite sustained increases in demand.

The overall systemic problem is that firms must try to reduce that proportion of their costs that are long-run costs relative to short-run costs. Firms then systematically unwind capacity, only investing in cases where to not would mean that what remains would be immediately obsolete even though it can be used and yield returns. This means that investments that are necessarily long run start to alter in unsystematic and unknowable but potentially damaging ways because these cannot be adjusted once incurred in the same manner that short-run costs are.

For example, if wages become intolerably high by some determination, then it is easy enough to restrict shifts to keep labour costs contained even if the level of wages cannot be altered. Alternatively, wages may well increase but people will turn up for work to find themselves fired the next day, as happened with the shambolic resolution to strikes in the platinum sector. Both achieve the same thing – they maintain the same overall cost level. And the rate of costs can be altered with relative ease if companies bothered, but of course that would imply withdrawing at a slower rate and what company wants to take that risk? This is not so simple for overhead costs because of their occurrence in the first instance but also how they can be distributed in the absence of increases in production.

Black Economic Empowerment

Black Economic Empowerment (BEE) allowed firms to resolve a pre-existing problem: how to dissolve and extract prior investment. What was incrementally better was to find a way to transfer any remaining liabilities – which constituted prior bad investments and which threatened to wipe these firms out – to someone else. Getting paid for a worthless pile in the process was the cherry on top. However, the problem really is not to inherit a worthless pile (it is bad, but would be salvageable simply by walking away and accepting having made a loss), it is that whether it will ever pay for itself since its 'owner' is now in hock and has just incurred the much bigger problem of having to work to make ballooning interest payments on a loan that will never be paid off.

That is, these liabilities are the high finance equivalent of mineworkers and farmer labourers who find themselves paying a constantly rising proportion of their income into the company or farmer's little tuck shop because he or she bought a can of beans.

Traditional capital is not merely spoilt, lazy and incompetent. It is destructive and anti-progressive wholesale. This rabid adherence to and defence of BEE by the new elite is in direct proportion to the extent to which they were paid a petty bribe to facilitate this process. It is however also proving to be in direct relation to a realisation that they were sold a dud and the real innovation was happening somewhere else, and with as much intrigue and distraction as a magic show. Unfortunately for capital, this game of smoke and mirrors is being exposed faster than it has taken to rob the grave. So the really interesting question then is whether to plan to buy substantially under-valued assets in a fire sale should capital simply just cut its losses and run, or whether the time for a more direct conflict has come should capital try to salvage whatever is left.

Investing in the elite has been the most unproductive and costly decision large firms historically operating in the South African market have made to date. BEE has proven more implicitly costly than even its own architects could have imagined. The first issue is the fracturing of the ANC-

SACP-COSATU Alliance and the second, within that, the monumental split within the ANC and COSATU themselves. The latter is arguably the more significant. Firms' planning has changed from a simpler need to appease an alliance with a single set of more-or-less uniform payments – since within the alliance a unitary set of demands would emerge because all disagreements would be settled internally – to having to incorporate and plan for considerably more scenarios. And if firms want to plan for all of these, they have no choice but to try to influence the range of interests that is proliferating.

CHAPTER 5

THE MANIFESTO FOR
SOCIAL CHANGE

Nothing has changed in South Africa in 350 years. There have been evolving forms of un-free labour, beginning with slavery, then indentured labour, and later a modified form of indenture under the migrant labour system that was developed – and built – the mining industry, and continues today.

All these systems of un-free labour are underwritten by endemic violence, which comes in various categories. First, there is the violence of the state and owners of capital against those who work, as we saw at Marikana. Second, there is the violence of the state towards the underclass, displayed in the cold-blooded killing by the police of Ficksburg community activist Andries Tatane in front of the world's cameras on 13 April 2011. Third, there is the counter-violence by the underclass, which can be seen in constantly erupting service delivery protests. Not only have these protests doubled to around 14 740 per year between 1997 and 2014, a rising proportion of them over the last few years has been classified by police as violent. And lastly, there is the internal violence within the underclass, caused by the pressure-cooker-like conditions under which they live.

Effectively, South Africa is a society with a hidden civil war. According to StatsSA, South Africa's murder rate in 2013/4 was 32.2 murders per 100 000 people. The global average murder rate for the same period was six murders per 100 000 people, according to research by the Institute for Security Studies. That is, South Africa has a murder rate that is over five times the global average – one of the highest of any country not currently at war.

All these forms of violence are inextricably linked to current economic activity in South Africa.

The consequence of South Africa's mode of economic operation since the mid-17th century has been the development of a large underclass. This group is not a reserve army of labour; that is, it is not related to the business cycle.

The individuals in the underclass never even get into the labour market. They are the product of the same instrument that created migrant labour in the first place, but they are not absorbed by the enterprises that created it.

The underclass has traditionally survived on remittances and been reproduced in this way over generations. The role remittances played was superseded by the grant system as the mining industry declined and the welfare state emerged. As a consequence, the underclass is economically marginalised, unskilled and not engaged in any significant commercial activity. They are largely dependent. This is a hugely unfavourable ecosystem to the worker. Because of its hostility toward the welfare of the worker, the ruling elite is anti-education as it sees this as a threat.

The society we found that most resembled South Africa today was Ancient Rome. Large numbers of people known as plebeians did not work; the work of the time was largely done by slaves. In order to sustain a large non-working population, the rulers conquered Western Europe, Asia Minor and North Africa. These conquered territories had to pay tribute to Rome, much of which was in the form of grain. This was what went into feeding the plebeians with free bread that was distributed by the Roman state.

Can this model work for South Africa today? No doubt there are perhaps leaders in the ANC government who think they can replicate the Roman conquests in southern Africa. The bad news for them is that this is no longer possible. For starters, the South African army is nowhere near having the capabilities of the Roman legions and, secondly, the people of Africa are now prepared to confront all foreign invaders.

The collective dynamic process of social change apparent in South Africa is intertwined with both the structural and cyclical elements of the violence directed at the underclass and the counter-violence by the underclass. Structurally, the underclass is a persistent and autonomously self-reproducing part of this society, and it essentially has a parallel existence that is completely outside of any formal domestic or international economic activity. That is, the underclass has an existence outside of the national economy.

This breeds these categories of violence as this situation is perpetuated. Cyclically, there is a fluctuating 'underclass activity cycle' during which the underclass is at times passive and at other times aggressive. This happens when the immediate environment and conditions of the underclass deteriorate, precipitating social unrest. There is a range of tangible and soft costs that are then associated with containing this agitation and restricting its spill-over into the formal structure of the economy and so into society at large.

'We can predict that we are going to be very busy in the several months leading up to the local elections, with community protests unfortunately diverting our human and physical resources,' Commissioner Riah Phiyega said during the police budget vote in May of 2015.

It is our argument that these costs explain the political transitions that have occurred in South African society while mired in an economy in which the characteristics and power relations are almost unchanged over the past four centuries.

The costs associated with the suppression of the underclass partly explain why political power has changed hands in South Africa from its early modern history through to the present day. When the administrative costs of control escalate beyond a sustainable level, the prevailing elite will rid themselves of these costs of control in order to protect and retain economic control.

Political power has consistently changed hands in South Africa whenever the previous incumbents have been faced with rising and unsustainable costs related to the suppression of the underclass. Power has simply been handed over to the next group to administer, conditional on the protection of the core economic interests of the prevailing elite.

The Dutch handed over to the British colonialists but retained the core agricultural interests of Afrikaner farmers. The British colonialists passed over control to the Afrikaner nationalists, contingent on mineral and finance interests remaining protected. The Afrikaner nationalists ceded

105

administrative control over to the African nationalists, contingent on the economic status quo being maintained, which essentially brings us to where South Africa is today.

The reason we have reached a deadlock is that, unlike former elites, the African nationalists are neither able nor willing to hand over control to the next administration. This is because the control of the state and its revenues is the means of sustenance of the current elite; the economic interest to be protected is contingent on and embedded in the control of political power. So the face-off between the underclass and the current ruling elite has arrived.

The result is that there is really no non-violent alternative as long as the social structure of South Africa remains, broadly, as it has for centuries. There are only different grades of this endemic violence embedded in any given alternative. Though undesirable, it is important to understand that even to maintain the status quo is an active, intentional choice. In the face of an unchanged social structure, we then have four potential scenarios.

The first is that we all passively step aside and let the situation as it stands in South Africa today play out to its logical conclusion. We would simply see more of what is happening today and on a larger scale. This is the necessary consequence of the current elite clinging to power.

The second alternative is that this hidden civil war erupts

into outright conflict as the underclass revolts, which would lead to anarchy. And when the state resists, it could lead to massacre.

The third alternative is what we would consider a more orderly and organised escalation in violence as either internal or external parties provide support for a violent insurrection by the underclass.

The fourth scenario, though stabilising, is still less than ideal, and the least likely. This society could simply agree to hand political power over to the underclass as a precursor to the underclass forming an economic coalition of its own choosing. That is, the political elite agree to diffuse power, but with an inbuilt responsibility attached to this right.

One means to this end is constitutional change to allow for constituency-based voting. Since we know it is not in the interest of the ruling party to acquiesce, then it is the quid pro quo that must form the basis of negotiation for any political coalition, which can now no longer subsume the interests of the underclass.

That is, while the endless political manoeuvring – as we vacillate from daydreams of an opposition that is inclusive of like-minded progressive South Africans (whatever that may mean) to ones of an opposition led by militants – may defer the onset of the escalation of the sort of conditions described above, it can only postpone the inevitable.

This includes doing away with the self-serving obscurantism of these so-called champions of the poor, amounting to a thinly veiled excuse to ascend to the reins of power and untold riches of assimilation into a corrupt and morally bankrupt system of governance that lacks credible checks and balances. Equate a more rapid transferal of political power to the underclass to ripping the plaster off in one swift motion. After all, this is the representative person of this society, and it is long overdue that this country's institutions fail to reflect this.

For South Africa to become and remain both productive and stable, it is necessary for the underclass to emerge from the prevailing system of perpetual bondage, breaking the deeply embedded social structure.

How the underclass gets and maintains political power is key. There must be an economic precursor to a political movement, so first it is necessary to mobilise the underclass through the injection of skills and capital into a productive environment; that is, strengthen the small-scale enterprises that they already run. This constitutes a move from being unskilled, idle and permanently dependent on remittances and social welfare to becoming viable commercial players. This effectively reproduces what would have happened had the mining industry not destroyed peasant agriculture through the migrant labour system.

In conjunction with this strategy, legislation could then, as a secondary mechanism, be used effectively to open up markets to small producers and/or cooperatives.

To acquire political power, the underclass must, on the one hand, merge with the sizeable contingent of blue-collar workers who are being spat out of formal work as employment is eroded in dying industries. On the other hand, they must also incorporate a segment of independent professionals whose fortune is independent of the status quo, which can also be part of the coalition.

This would constitute the political arm of a new movement for the re-industrialisation of South Africa through the promotion of new industries. And from this would emerge new partnerships between any scale of new industry/businesses and the underclass, which is essentially an untrained potential labour force. The underclass has to independently have the political power to persuade industrialists to be their allies, and this political power consists of the ability to remove obstacles to the establishment of new industries. In particular, it consists of the ability to eliminate the legislation that protects, if not promotes, the tendency for cartelisation in production in the South African economy.

In short, the only way to save South Africa is for the underclass to control the state albeit in coalition with sections of the various social classes as outlined above.

STATISTICS SOUTH AFRICA

BREAKDOWN OF
SOCIAL CLASSES

Economic and political elite and middle class (2005)

This category is made up of individuals who earn R6 684 or more per month. The category excludes professionals who work for themselves and those individuals who are working for non-profit organisations.

Population group	Public sector*	A co-operative, self-help association, labour union, professional association or business league	Private sector**	Total
Elite (above R34 676 per month)				
Black African	11 042	1 555	3 626	16 223
Coloured	79		4 552	4 631
Indian/Asian			2 513	2 513
White	5 963	2 323	44 943	53 229
Total	**17 084**	**3 878**	**55 633**	**76 596**
Middle class (above R6 684 but less than R34 676 per month)				
Black African	299 808	4 013	222 355	526 176
Coloured	70 015	3 388	70 857	144 261
Indian/Asian	21 104	1 683	68 328	91 115
White	175 055	8 901	523 044	707 239
Total	**565 982**	**17 986**	**884 583**	**1 468 791**

*Includes government-controlled businesses, such as Eskom/Telkom
**Includes people who work in private households

Blue-collar workers/lower middle class (2005)

This category includes all individuals working in the formal sector who earn less than R6 684 a month, excluding professionals who work for themselves and those individuals who are employed in non-profit organisations.

Population group	Formal sector
Black African	4 729 742
Coloured	1 065 940
Indian/Asian	292 679
White	1 093 314
Total	**7 181 675**

Underclass workers and the unemployed (2005)

This category includes all individuals who work in the informal sector and earning less than R6 684 a month, excluding professionals who work for themselves and those individuals who are employed in non-profit organisations.

Population group	Employed in the informal sector	Unemployed	Total
Black African	3 366 237	5 518 400	8 884 638
Coloured	227 739	538 182	765 921
Indian/Asian	33 588	102 020	135 608
White	74 494	175 552	250 046
Total	**3 702 058**	**6 334 154**	**10 036 212**

113

Independent professionals and those working for non-profit organisations (2005)

This category includes professionals working for themselves and individuals working in non-profit organisations.

Population group	Employed in the informal sector	Unemployed	Total
Black African	95 013	96 711	191 724
Coloured	4 730	11 620	16 350
Indian/Asian	7 417	2 493	9 910
White	81 681	25 663	107 344
Total	**188 841**	**136 487**	**325 328**

Economic and political elite and middle class (2010)

This category is made up of individuals who earn R9 298 or more per month. The category excludes professionals who work for themselves and those individuals who are working for non-profit organisations.

Population group	Public sector*	Private sector**	Total
Elite (above R48 241 per month)			
Black African	8 894	13 208	22 102
Coloured	1 709	2 800	4 508
Indian/Asian	192	12 516	12 709
White	6 246	55 279	61 525
Total	**17 041**	**83 803**	**100 844**
Middle class (above R9 298 but less than R48 241 per month)			
Black African	492 964	480 150	973 114
Coloured	68 102	129 815	197 918
Indian/Asian	34 925	132 255	167 180
White	174 271	813 741	988 012
Total	**770 262**	**1 555 961**	**2 326 223**

*Includes government-controlled businesses, such as Eskom/Telkom
**Includes people who work in private households

Blue-collar workers/lower middle class (2010)

This category includes all individuals working in the formal sector who earn less than R9 298 a month, excluding professionals who work for themselves and those individuals who are employed in non-profit organisations.

Population group	Formal sector
Black African	5 543 411
Coloured	1 075 208
Indian/Asian	288 212
White	888 375
Total	**7 795 207**

Underclass workers and the unemployed (2010)

This category includes all individuals who work in the informal sector and earning less than R9 298 a month, excluding professionals who work for themselves and those individuals who are employed in non-profit organisations.

Population group	Employed in the informal sector	Unemployed	Total
Black African	3 017 192	6 758 879	9 776 072
Coloured	241 201	550 677	791 879
Indian/Asian	37 218	70 473	107 690
White	64 567	178 366	242 933
Total	**3 360 178**	**7 558 395**	**10 918 573**

Independent professionals and those working for non-profit organisations (2010)

This category includes professionals working for themselves and individuals working in non-profit organisations.

Population group	Independent professionals	Working for NGOs	Total
Black African	100 661	77 716	178 376
Coloured	10 684	16 454	27 138
Indian/Asian	7 435	823	8 259
White	115 279	27 600	142 879
Total	**234 059**	**122 593**	**356 652**

Economic and political elite and middle class (2014)

This category is made up of individuals who earn R11 565 or more per month. The category excludes professionals who work for themselves and those individuals who are working for non-profit organisations.

Population group	Public sector*	Private sector**	NGO	Total
Elite (above R60 000 per month)				
Black African	9 881	27 288		37 169
Coloured	2 448	6 356	124	8 804
Indian/Asian		4 664		4 644
White	7 941	46 459	818	54 400
Total	**20 270**	**84 766**	**943**	**105 036**
Middle class (above R11 565 but less than R60 000 per month)				
Black African	549 614	697 826	8 853	1 247 440
Coloured	57 864	172 349	1 924	230 213
Indian/Asian	17 744	89 162	960	106 905
White	108 492	597 165	14 508	705 657
Total	**733 713**	**1 556 502**	**26 245**	**2 290 215**

*Includes government-controlled businesses, such as Eskom/Telkom
**Includes people who work in private households

Blue-collar workers/lower middle class (2014)

This category includes all individuals working in the formal sector who earn less than R11 565 a month, excluding professionals who work for themselves and those individuals who are employed in non-profit organisations.

Population group	Formal sector
Black African	6 507 152
Coloured	1 119 414
Indian/Asian	330 225
White	1 048 669
Total	**9 005 460**

Underclass workers and the unemployed (2014)

This category includes all individuals who work in the informal sector and earning less than R11 565 a month, excluding professionals who work for themselves and those individuals who are employed in non-profit organisations.

Population group	Employed in the informal sector	Unemployed	Total
Black African	3 109 295	7 336 801	10 446 096
Coloured	243 044	632 114	875 158
Indian/Asian	48 135	101 404	149 539
White	81 449	203 502	284 951
Total	**3 481 923**	**8 273 821**	**11 755 744**

Independent professionals and those working for non-profit organisations (2014)

This category includes professionals working for themselves and individuals working in non-profit organisations.

Population group	Independent professionals	Working for NGOs	Total
Black African	108 348	142 107	250 455
Coloured	12 368	20 133	32 500
Indian/Asian	7 716	5 156	12 872
White	106 412	29 277	135 690
Total	**234 844**	**196 673**	**431 517**

Summary: Social structure (2005, 2010 and 2014)

	2005	2010	2014	A co-operative, self-help association, labour union, professional association or business league in 2005. (This is due to different classification used in 2005.)
Elite				
Economic	55 633	83 803	84 766	3 878
Political	17 084	17 041	20 270	17 986
Middle class				
Economic	884 583	1 555 961	1 556 502	
Political	565 982	770 262	753 984	
Blue-collar workers/lower middle class	7 181 675	7 792 207	9 005 460	
Underclass and unemployed	10 036 212	10 918 573	11 755 744	
Independent professionals and non-profit organisations	325 328	356 652	431 517	

NOTES

The notes that follow are from Chapter 4: 'How Capital is Complicit in Economic Stagnation'. The complete reference for each of the authors and titles referred to can be found in the Select Bibliography.

1 Trapido, 1971.

2 cf. Ramamurti, 2008; Goldstein, 2009.

3 Cowling and Sugden, 1998; Dunn, 2001.

4 cf. Steindl, 1952.

5 cf. Giliomee, 2008.

6 cf. Potts, 2001; Earl and Wakeley, 2012.

7 Lewis, 1995; Bell, 1995; Fedderke et al., 2007; Fedderke and Szalontai, 2009.

8 Kalecki, 1954; 1971; Sawyer, 1995; Galbraith, 1967; Shapiro, 2011; 2012; Dunn, 2011.

9 cf. Galbraith, 1967; Eichner, 1976; 1987; Dunn, 2011; Shapiro and Mott, 2005; Shapiro and Sawyer, 2003.

10 cf. Kalecki, 1954; 1971; Sawyer, 1983; 1982; Lavoie, 1992; 2006.

SELECT BIBLIOGRAPHY

Aghion, P., M. Braun and J. Fedderke. 2008. 'Competition and Productivity Growth in South Africa'. *Economics of Transition*, Volume 16, Issue 4, pp.741–768.

Aghion, P., J. Fedderke, P. Howitt and N. Viegi. 2013. 'Testing Creative Destruction in an Opening Economy: the Case of the South African Manufacturing Industries'. *Economics of Transition*, Volume 21, Issue 3, pp.419–450.

Baran, P. and P. Sweezy. 1966. *Monopoly Capital: An Essay on the American Economic and Social Order*. New York, Monthly Review Press.

Bell, T. 'Improving Manufacturing Performance in South Africa: A Contrary View'. 1995. *Transformation*, Volume 28, pp.1–34.

Biesebroeck, J. 2005. 'Firm Size Matters: Growth and Productivity Growth in African Manufacturing'. *Economic Development and Cultural Change*, Volume 53, Issue 3, pp.545–583.

Cape Blue Book, G27–1874, 1874, Cape Town.

Chapman, C. 1872. *A Voyage from Southampton to Cape Town, in the Union Company's Mail Steamer*. G. Berridge & Co.

Commons, J.R. 1950. *The Economics of Collective Action*. New York, Macmillan.

Correia, C. and P. Cramer. 2008. 'An Analysis of Cost of Capital, Capital Structure and Capital Budgeting Practices: A Survey of South African Listed Companies'. *Meditari Accountancy Research*, Volume 16, No. 1, pp.31–52.

Cowling, K. 1982. *Monopoly Capitalism*. London, Macmillan.

Cowling, K. and R. Sugden. 1998. 'The Essence of the Modern Corporation: Markets, Strategic Decision-Making and the Theory of the Firm'. *The Manchester School*, Volume 66, No. 1, pp.59–86.

Davenport, J. 2013. *Digging Deep: A History in South Africa 1852–2002*. Cape Town, Jonathan Ball Publishers.

Davidson, P. 1999. *Uncertainty, International Money, Employment and Theory: The Collected Writings of Paul Davidson*. Basingstoke, Macmillan.

———. 2007. *John Maynard Keynes*. Basingstoke, Palgrave Macmillan.

Dunn, S.P. 2001. 'Bounded Rationality is not Fundamental Uncertainty: A Post Keynesian Perspective'. *Journal of Post Keynesian Economics*. Volume 23, Issue 4, pp.567–587.

———. 2011. *The Economics of John Kenneth Galbraith: Introduction, Persuasion and Rehabilitation*. Cambridge, Cambridge University Press.

Earl, P.E. and T. Wakeley. 2012. 'Alternative Perspectives on Connections in Economic Systems'. *Journal of Evolutionary Economics*, Volume 20, pp.163–183.

Eichner, A.S. 1976. *The Megacorp and Oligopoly: Microfoundations of Macrodynamics*. Cambridge, Cambridge University Press.

————. 1987. *The Macrodynamics of Advanced Market Economies*. New York, M.E. Sharpe.

Fedderke, J.W. and Z. Bogetic. 'Infrastructure and Growth in South Africa: Direct and Indirect Productivity Impacts of 19 Infrastructure Measures'. *World Development*, Volume 37, No. 9, pp.1522–1539.

Fedderke, J., C. Kularatne and M. Mariotti. 2007. 'Mark-up Pricing in South African Industry'. *Journal of African Economies*. Volume 16, Issue 1, pp.28–69.

Fedderke, J. and D. Naumann. 2011. 'An Analysis of Concentration in South African Manufacturing, 1972–2001'. *Applied Economics*, Volume 43, pp.2919–2939.

Fedderke, J. and S. Schirmer, 2007. 'The R&D Performance of the South African Manufacturing Sector, 1970–1993'. *Economic Change and Restructuring*, Volume 39, pp.125–151.

Fedderke, J. and G. Szalontai. 2009. 'Industry Concentration in South African Manufacturing: Trends and Consequences, 1972–96'. *Economic Modelling*, Volume 26, pp.241–250.

Galbraith, J.K. 1967. *The New Industrial State*. London, André Deutsch Ltd, second edition, 1972.

————. 1983. *The Anatomy of Power*. Boston, Houghton Mifflin.

Giddens, A. 1984. *The Constitution of Society: Outline of the Theory of Structurisation*. Cambridge, Polity.

Giliomee, H. 2008. 'Ethnic Business and Economic Empowerment: The Afrikaner Case, 1915–1970'. *South African Journal of Economics*, Volume 76, Issue 4, pp.765–788.

Goldstein, A. 2009. 'Multinational Companies from Emerging

Economies Composition, Conceptualization and Direction in the Global Economy'. *Indian Journal of Industrial Relations*. Volume 45, No. 1, pp.137–147.

Hodgson, G.M. 1998. 'The Approach of Institutional Economics'. *Journal of Economic Literature*, Volume XXXVI, pp.166–192.

———. 2015. *Conceptualizing Capitalism: Institutions, Evolution, Future.* Chicago, University of Chicago Press.

Journal of Southern African Studies, Volume 37, Issue 1, 2011, London

Kalecki, M. 1954. *Theory of Economic Dynamics: An Essay on Cyclical and Long-Run Changes in Capitalist Economy*. London, George Allen & Unwin, revised second edition, 1965.

———. 1971. *Selected Essays on the Dynamics of the Capitalist Economy: 1933–1970.* Cambridge, Cambridge University Press.

Kay, N.M. 1976. *The Innovating Firm: A Behavioural Theory of Corporate R&D*. New York, St Martin's Press.

———. 1982. *The Evolving Firm: Strategy and Structure in Industrial Organization*. New York, St Martin's Press.

———. 1997. *Pattern in Corporate Evolution*. Oxford, Oxford University Press.

Keynes, J.M. 1936. *The General Theory of Employment, Interest and Money*, in *The Collected Writings of John Maynard Keynes: Volume VII*. D.E. Moggridge (ed). Cambridge, Cambridge University Press, 1973.

Lavoie, M. 1992. *Foundations of Post-Keynesian Economic Analysis*. Aldershot, Edward Elgar Publishing Ltd.

———. 2006. *Introduction to Post-Keynesian Economics*. Basingstoke,

Palgrave Macmillan.

Lind, M. 2012. *Land of Promise: An Economic History of the United States*, New York, HarperCollins.

Mandela, N. 1995. *Long Walk to Freedom*. London, Abacus.

Mbeki, M. July 1981. 'The African Middle Class and Political Change in South Africa, 1884–1994'. Unpublished Master of Arts Dissertation. Coventry, University of Warwick.

Moore, B. 1988. *Horizontalists and Verticalists: The Macroeconomics of Credit Money*. New York, Cambridge University Press.

Nattrass, N. 1991. 'Controversies about Capitalism and Apartheid in South Africa: An Economic Perspective'. *Journal of South African Studies*, Volume 17, Issue 4, pp.654–677.

Nkosi, M. 2011. *Mining Deep: The Origins of the Labour Structure in South Africa*. Cape Town, David Philip.

Ojah, K. and K. Pillay. 2009. 'Debt Markets and Corporate Debt Structure in an Emerging Market: The South African Example', *Economic Modelling*, Volume 26, pp.1215–1227.

Potts, J. 2001. 'Uncertainty, Complexity and Imagination', in Earl and Frowen (eds). *Economics as an Art of Thought: Essays in Memory of G.L.S. Shackle*. London, Routledge.

Ramamurti, R. 2008. 'What Have We Learned About Emerging Market MNEs? Insights from a Multi-country Research Project'. Presentation given at The Conference on Emerging Multinationals: Outward FDI from Emerging and Developing Countries, Copenhagen Business School, Copenhagen, Denmark. http://www.gdex.dk/ofdi/68%20 Ramamurti%20Ravi.pdf (accessed on 31 July 2015).

Tool, M.R. and W.J. Samuels. 1989. *The Economy as a System of Power*. Piscataway, Transaction Publishers.

Tool, M.R. and W.J. Samuels (eds). 1989. *State, Society and Corporate Power*. Piscataway, Transaction Publishers, second edition.

Sawyer, M.C. 1981. *The Economics of Industries and Firms*. London, Routledge, second edition.

———. 1982. *Macroeconomics in Question: The Keynesian-Monetarist Orthodoxies and the Kaleckian Alternative*. Brighton, Wheatsheaf.

———. 1983. *Business Pricing and Inflation*. London, Macmillan.

———. 1985. *The Economics of Michał Kalecki*. Radical Economics Series. London, Macmillan.

———. 1995. *Unemployment, Imperfect Competition and Macroeconomics: Essays in the Post-Keynesian Tradition*. Aldershot, Edward Elgar Publishing Ltd.

———. 1996. 'Kalecki on the Trade Cycle and Economic Growth', in J.E. King (ed). *An Alternative Macroeconomic Theory: The Kaleckian Model and Post-Keynesian Economics*. Recent Economic Thought Series. London, Kluwer Academic Publishers.

Shackle, G.L.S. 1961. *Decision, Order and Time in Human Affairs*. Cambridge, Cambridge University Press, second edition, 1969.

Shapiro, N. 1990. 'The "Megacorp": Eichner's Contribution to the Theory of the Firm'. *Journal of Economic Issues*, Volume XXIV, No. 2, pp.493–500.

———. 1994. 'Competition', in Arestis, P. and M. Sawyer (eds). *The Elgar Companion to Radical Political Economy*. Cheltenham, Edward Elgar Publishing Ltd, second edition.

———. 2011. 'The Function of Firms: Alternative Views', in P. Arestis (ed). *Microeconomics, Macroeconomics and Economic Policy: Essays in Honour of Malcolm Sawyer*. Basingstoke, Palgrave Macmillan.

Shapiro N. and Mott, T. (eds). 2005. *Rethinking Capitalist Development: Essays on the Economics of Josef Steindl*. London, Routledge.

Shapiro, N. and M. Sawyer. 2003. 'Post-Keynesian Price Theory'. *Journal of Post-Keynesian Economics*, Volume 25, Issue 3, pp.355–65.

Steindl, J. 1952. *Maturity and Stagnation in American Capitalism*. Oxford University Institute of Statistics Monographs. Number 4. Oxford, Basil Blackwell.

———. 1990. 'Trend and Cycle', in N. Shapiro and T. Mott (eds). *Rethinking Capitalist Development: Essays on the Economics of Josef Steindl*. London, Routledge.

Trapido, S. 1971. 'South Africa in a Comparative Study of Industrialization'. *The Journal of Development Studies*, Volume 7, Issue 3, pp.309–320.

Tregenna, F. 2012. 'Sources of Subsectoral Growth in South Africa', *Oxford Development Studies*, Volume 40, Issue 2, pp.162–189.

Van Onselen, C. 2005. *The Seed in Maine: The Life of Kas Mine – A South African Sharecropper*. Cape Town, Jonathan Ball Publishers.

Veblen, T. 1899. *The Theory of the Leisure Class*. London, George Allen & Unwin, 1970.

———. 1919. *The Vested Interests and the Common Man*. New York, Augustus M. Kelley, new edition, 1975.

Welsh, F. 2000. *A History of South Africa*. London, HarperCollins.